OECD Reviews of Vocational Education and Training

Apprenticeship and Vocational Education and Training in Israel

Małgorzata Kuczera, Tanja Bastianić and Simon Field

This work is published under the responsibility of the Secretary-General of the OECD. The opinions expressed and arguments employed herein do not necessarily reflect the official views of OECD member countries.

This document, as well as any data and any map included herein, are without prejudice to the status of or sovereignty over any territory, to the delimitation of international frontiers and boundaries and to the name of any territory, city or area.

Please cite this publication as:
Kuczera, M., T. Bastianić and S. Field (2018), *Apprenticeship and Vocational Education and Training in Israel*, OECD Reviews of Vocational Education and Training, OECD Publishing, Paris.
http://dx.doi.org/10.1787/9789264302051-en

ISBN 978-92-64-30204-4 (print)
ISBN 978-92-64-30205-1 (PDF)

Series: OECD Reviews of Vocational Education and Training
ISSN 2077-7728 (print)
ISSN 2077-7736 (online)

The statistical data for Israel are supplied by and under the responsibility of the relevant Israeli authorities. The use of such data by the OECD is without prejudice to the status of the Golan Heights, East Jerusalem and Israeli settlements in the West Bank under the terms of international law.

Photo credits: Cover © LituFalco - Fotolia.com.

Corrigenda to OECD publications may be found on line at: *www.oecd.org/about/publishing/corrigenda.htm*.
© OECD 2018

You can copy, download or print OECD content for your own use, and you can include excerpts from OECD publications, databases and multimedia products in your own documents, presentations, blogs, websites and teaching materials, provided that suitable acknowledgment of the source and copyright owner(s) is given. All requests for public or commercial use and translation rights should be submitted to *rights@oecd.org*. Requests for permission to photocopy portions of this material for public or commercial use shall be addressed directly to the Copyright Clearance Center (CCC) at *info@copyright.com* or the Centre francais d'exploitation du droit de copie (CFC) at *contact@cfcopies.com*.

Foreword

Israel has experienced strong economic growth over the last decade, and unemployment is now below 5%. Skills shortages are emerging in several technical areas. If Israel is to meet the demand for skills and to support its economic growth it can either increase external migration or/and use its education and training system more effectively. At the same time, inequity and disadvantage in some population groups are raising the profile of other demands for vocational training as a vehicle for social inclusion. Collectively, these factors are driving policy interest in developing a vocational education and training (VET) system which is currently both fragmented and of modest scale when compared with the VET systems of other OECD countries.

This OECD report *Apprenticeship and Vocational Education and Training in Israel* compares the VET policy in Israeli with practice in other countries, and on this basis draws policy conclusions. Among others, the report argues for the expansion and integration of apprenticeship programmes into the mainstream upper-secondary system; development of systematic work-based learning in selected school-based VET programmes; support of employers with provision of high-quality work-based learning; setting up a national strategic body to plan and guide policy development in VET; and, focus on literacy and numeracy in VET programmes for young people and for adults.

This report was drafted by Małgorzata Kuczera, Tanja Bastianić and Simon Field. Elisa Larrakoetxea and Jennifer Cannon provided valuable administrative support. The OECD is very grateful to colleagues in Israel, in the Ministry of Labour and Social Affairs and many other people we met during our visits for their many very constructive contributions to the review. In particular we are grateful to Shmuel Pur and Lior Zysev-Yogev from the Ministry of Labour and Social Affairs; Yaakov Sheinbaum from the Ministry of Education; Sophie Artsev and Haim Portnoy from the Central Bureau of Statistics; Judith King, Nir Levy and Tirza Willner from Myers-JDC-Brookdale. Within the OECD the report benefited from many helpful comments and advice from Francois Keslair, Anthony Mann, Marco Paccagnella and William Thorn in the Directorate for Education and Skills and Claude Giorno and Gabriel Machlica from the Economics Department.

Table of contents

Executive summary 9

1. Assessment and recommendations 11
    Introduction 12
    The education system of Israel 14
    Israel's vocational education and training system 16
    Policy development 19
    Assessment: Strengths and challenges 20
    Policy options 22
    References 26

2. Developing work-based learning in Israel 29
    Introduction: Building work-based learning in different contexts 30
    Policy options: Developing work-based learning for young people and adults 34
    Policy arguments: The rationale for reform 34
    References 45

3. A closer look at the economics of training in Israel: Involving employers through youth apprenticeship and sectoral training levies 47
    Introduction: How to engage employers? 48
    Policy option 3.1: Making apprenticeships attractive to employers 50
    Policy arguments: The rationale for reform 51
    Policy option 3.2: Sharing cost of training among employers 56
    Policy arguments: The rationale for reform 56
    References 61

4. Creating a coherent and transparent vocational education and training system in Israel 63
    Introduction: Why coherence and transparency matter 64
    Policy option 4.1: Realising coherence in governance 64
    Policy arguments: The rationale for reform 65
    Policy option 4.2: Developing post-secondary options 69
    Policy arguments: The rationale for reform 70
    References 75

5. Improving literacy and numeracy in vocational education and training (VET) programmes in Israel 77
    Introduction: Comparing basic skills in Israel with other countries 78
    Policy options: Addressing basic skills challenge in VET and apprenticeship programmes 80
    Policy arguments: The rationale for reform 80
    References 89

Tables

Table 1.1. Participation of different ministries in training 18
Table 2.1. The duration of apprenticeship programmes and how apprentices spend their time 31
Table 2.2. Vocational programmes for adults involving work-based learning 33
Table 3.1. Costs and benefits associate with skilled and unskilled work of apprentices 49
Table 3.2. Minimum apprentice wages in youth apprenticeships 52
Table 3.3. How the minimum apprentice wage is determined 53
Table 3.4. Financial incentives to companies providing apprenticeships 57
Table 4.1. Funding of practical engineering and technician programmes and 'academic' engineers ... 73

Figures

Figure 1.1. Use of computers by blue-collar workers 22
Figure 2.1. In Israel, more young people aspire to skilled jobs than in most other countries 37
Figure 2.2. Share of upper-secondary VET graduates enrolled in education 38
Figure 2.3. In Israel, there is limited evidence for a wage premium from technological education 39
Figure 2.4. More than half of Israel's upper-secondary VET graduates see their job as unqualified ... 40
Figure 3.1. Allocation of apprentices to skilled and unskilled work in Switzerland and Austria 50
Figure 3.2. On-the-job training 59
Figure 3.3. Provision of training in Israel, by company size 60
Figure 5.1. Israel has a higher proportion of low-skilled adults than most countries 79
Figure 5.2. Share of low-skilled and absolute numbers in different population groups 79
Figure 5.3. The Israeli workforce includes a large share of low-skilled 81
Figure 5.4. In Israel, VET upper-secondary graduates have a low average and a wide spread of numeracy performance 83
Figure 5.5. Share of employed by skills and population group 85

Boxes

Box 1.1. The main conclusions from Skills beyond School, the OECD's review of post-secondary vocational education and training in Israel, published 2014 13
Box 1.2. The school networks in Israel 17
Box 2.1. Analysis of outcomes from upper-secondary VET in Israel, with the Survey of Adult Skills 37
Box 2.2. Incentive measures for adult apprentices 44
Box 3.1. Country examples of training for apprentice supervisors in the workplace 54
Box 3.2. Sectoral training levies in Switzerland 58
Box 4.1. Community colleges in the United States 71
Box 5.1. Innovative initiatives addressing poor basic skills in US colleges 87

Follow OECD Publications on:

http://twitter.com/OECD_Pubs

http://www.facebook.com/OECDPublications

http://www.linkedin.com/groups/OECD-Publications-4645871

http://www.youtube.com/oecdilibrary

http://www.oecd.org/oecddirect/

This book has...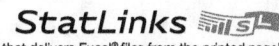

A service that delivers Excel® files from the printed page!

Look for the *StatLinks* at the bottom of the tables or graphs in this book. To download the matching Excel® spreadsheet, just type the link into your Internet browser, starting with the *http://dx.doi.org* prefix, or click on the link from the e-book edition.

Executive summary

In coming years Israel will need to invest substantially in skills, given a growing economy, a wave of retirements among technically trained immigrants from the former Soviet Union, low labour force participation in some sub-populations, and continuing problems with weak labour productivity. Collectively, these factors undermine the Israeli economy and social cohesion.

Key findings

By international standards Israel has many jobs requiring high-level skills and few elementary low-skilled occupations. While this shows that the Israeli economy is particularly dependent on the supply of highly skilled labour, labour shortages are observed in many sectors and occupations. If Israel is to meet the demand for skills and to support its economic growth it can either increase external migration or/and use its education and training system more effectively to respond to labour market needs. Vocational education and training (VET) in Israel can effectively support the Israeli economy by providing the skills in demand on the labour market as well as improving the life chances of individuals.

Key messages

Developing work-based learning

The current school-based VET system serves some students well by providing them with strong academic skills and preparing them well for entry to university. But others are left behind. These are students who do not pass matriculation exams (Bagrut), who drop out during the programme, and who do not continue to higher levels of education for other reasons. These students face uncertain labour market benefits. Reforms are needed to better integrate apprenticeship and work-based learning into upper-secondary VET. They should be part of the mainstream provision, rather than an option for potential drop-outs. This would involve an expansion of apprenticeship programmes, and development of systematic work-based learning placements in selected school-based VET programmes. The requirement of a special exemption to enter an apprenticeship should be dropped.

For adults, diverse work-based learning measures, including apprenticeship may help to alleviate skills shortages and integrate disadvantaged social groups into the labour market. To expand apprenticeship programmes for adults, Israel should devise incentive and support measures based on analysis of relevant costs and benefits for different target groups e.g. by gender, minority status and age.

Involving employers through youth apprenticeship and sectoral training levies

The support of employers is necessary to reform vocational programmes, including expansion of work-based learning in VET. Experience from other countries shows that programmes with longer work placements, such as apprenticeship, are often used by employers as a recruitment tool. Currently many employers in Israel are not able to realise long-term benefits associated with recruitment of the most able apprentices because many young apprentices enter the military service after completing apprenticeship programmes. When apprentices are rapidly trained and placed in skilled productive work apprenticeships can also yield large short-term benefits to employers. Apprenticeships leading to net benefits in the short term can therefore be particularly attractive to employers in Israel.

Low productivity and skills shortages in several economic sectors are holding back Israel's economic growth. While employers would collectively benefit from more workforce training, it is not always in the individual interest of an employer to offer training. To overcome this barrier, and create the step change necessary to improve the supply of skills, Israel may wish to support the establishment of sectoral training levies initiated by social partners (employers and trade unions). This is an approach which has been used successfully in some European countries.

Creating a coherent and transparent system

The vocational system needs to be internally coherent, with clear relationships between different VET programmes, and clear routes of transfer and progression between vocational training and general education programmes. This allows individuals to make choices between vocational programmes and helps employers to understand and relate to the different vocational programmes. To make the system more coherent, Israel should create a single strategic body that will plan and guide policy development on vocational education and training, and champion VET within government. A national qualification framework would also make the system more coherent and transparent.

In Israel many young people fail to obtain the Bagrut and many do not enter higher education. The offer for these young people is currently weak and underfunded if compared to other post-secondary options. Israel's economic performance and social cohesion depends on giving these young people relevant working skills and integrating them into the labour market. Israel may consider expanding and diversifying provision at post-secondary level, and promote pathways so that vocational choices are not dead ends.

Improving literacy and numeracy in VET programmes

Basic skills of numeracy and literacy have a major impact on life chances. They are positively associated with a range of important economic and social outcomes both for individuals and countries. In Israel, a large share of young people leave initial VET with poor basic skills. Israel should therefore ensure adequate levels of literacy and numeracy in all students, identifying the weakest performers and targeting teaching resources on them to improve performance. One practical step to this end would be to build into all vocational programmes, including youth apprenticeship and technological programmes, increased attention to the basic skills of numeracy and literacy.

In Israel around one in three of those in work have low numeracy or literacy skills, more than most other OECD countries. To tackle this challenge, Israel should also give consideration to building basic skills education systematically into adult programmes. Basic skills are particularly low among Arab Israelis and Haredi Jews. These populations are also less likely to participate in the labour market and are more at risk of living in poverty. Since basic skills are closely related to the labour market outcomes and life chances, addressing basis skills weaknesses in these populations should be a priority.

Chapter 1. Assessment and recommendations

> *This chapter describes the main characteristics of Israeli apprenticeship and vocational education and training (VET), and recent policy developments in Israel. It assesses the strengths of the system, the challenges that remain, and summarises suggestions for policy advanced in depth in later chapters of the report. Subsequent chapters examine different topics by introducing a challenge experienced by VET in Israel, advancing policy suggestions, providing arguments for the proposed policy solutions and discussing how these policy solutions could be implemented in the Israeli context.*

The statistical data for Israel are supplied by and under the responsibility of the relevant Israeli authorities. The use of such data by the OECD is without prejudice to the status of the Golan Heights, East Jerusalem and Israeli settlements in the West Bank under the terms of international law.

Introduction

Multiple factors are focusing attention on the development of vocational education and training (VET)

In Israel, several issues are intensifying attention on the provision of vocational training. Despite the global economic crisis, Israel has experienced strong economic growth over the last decade, and unemployment is now below 5%. Skills shortages are emerging in several technical areas, exacerbated by a wave of retirements by many of the technically trained personnel who migrated to Israel from the former Soviet Union 20 years ago. In response, employers are pressing for an expansion of skills training and work-based learning, and the government has launched a number of initiatives to this end. At the same time, inequity and disadvantage in some population groups are raising the profile of other demands for vocational training as a vehicle for social inclusion. Collectively, these factors are driving policy interest in developing a VET system which is currently both fragmented and of modest scale when compared with the VET systems of other OECD countries.

Inequality remains a major challenge

Both the Haredi and Arab populations have high poverty rates, with at least half of the Arab population and 60% of the Haredi population below the poverty line (OECD, 2010a). Both groups have had high birth rates. A long-standing anxiety about low rates of economic activity among Haredi men and Arab women has eased slightly in the last few years, but the challenge of targeting vocational training on these two groups in a way that will transition them into work remains significant. While there are special issues in encouraging employment among these different groups, VET is a key means to this end, with the aim not just of realising insertion into the labour market, but also of launching rewarding careers that will help to improve social cohesion.

The point of departure for this review was a previous OECD study

The 2014 OECD review of VET in Israel (the conclusions are reported in Box 1.1), looked primarily at post-secondary VET. More recent developments include new initiatives on apprenticeship and work-based learning, further studies by international bodies (OECD, 2018a), and a significant new report by the Israeli National Economic Council encouraging a more co-ordinated VET system. This OECD review builds on this sequence of work. It is one of a series of OECD studies of VET and apprenticeship systems in more than 40 countries, and draws on the extensive experience of the OECD in these areas, as well as The Survey of Adult Skills, a product of the Programme for the International Assessment of Adult Competencies (PIAAC), in which Israel participated, and which examined the numeracy, literacy and digital skills of adults (16-65 year-olds). As a contribution to this work, a background report was prepared on behalf of the Israeli authorities (Ben Rabi et al., forthcoming). The OECD team undertook two missions to Israel in December 2016 and in May 2017, and met and held discussions with a wide range of stakeholders, including the Ministry of Education (MoE) as well as the Ministry of Labour, Welfare and Social Services (MLWSS) which sponsored this exercise, other interested ministries, employers and trade union groups, and made visits to several vocational training institutions. This review draws extensively on these discussions.

Box 1.1. The main conclusions from Skills beyond School, the OECD's review of post-secondary vocational education and training in Israel, published 2014

Strengths

- The post-secondary system is diverse, including not only practical engineering and technician training and vocational courses, but also professional certifications, private courses, and targeted programmes directed at disadvantaged groups.

- There is an active framework of government-led reform. The social partners – both employers and unions – are well organised and are keen to engage.

- The certification system provides an effective means of upskilling.

- Although data remain a challenge, research and analysis are well developed by international standards.

Challenges and recommendations

- Growing skills challenges threaten the Israeli economy: **Launch a strategic expansion of high-quality vocational education and training programmes, guided by partnership with industry, and underpinned by legislation. Make the vocational skills learnt during the military service more transparent and transferable.**

- Uncoordinated governance systems make the system difficult to navigate for students. **Establish a national body involving all the key stakeholders to provide strategic guidance on the development of the VET system.**

- Work-based learning is little used. **Integrate work-based learning systematically into post-secondary vocational programmes.**

- Graduates of vocational tracks often face obstacles to further learning. **Improve the access of upper-secondary VET graduates to further learning opportunities, including post-secondary VET; and enhance access to universities and credit recognition for graduates of practical engineering programmes.**

- Effective vocational teachers need to have pedagogical skills, and professional expertise. **Pursue reforms in the practical engineering and technician programmes to allow people with work experience to enter teaching. Design initial teacher education programmes so as to ensure a good mix of pedagogical skills, vocational competence and industry knowledge. Converge the entry requirements and training programmes for all teachers of practical engineering programmes to a common standard.**

Source: Musset, P., M. Kuczera and S. Field (2014), *A Skills beyond School Review of Israel*, OECD Reviews of Vocational Education and Training, http://dx.doi.org/10.1787/9789264210769-en.

Some of the recommendations of the OECD's 2014 review have now been implemented

The skills learnt by young people during their military service are now being certified, supporting their future training and return to civilian life. The proposal to establish a national qualifications framework has been taken up in the report of the National Economic Council, which is also exploring the pathways for practical engineering graduates to pursue engineering and other degree level qualifications in universities. OECD recommendations on the development of work-based learning have been implemented in the shape of a new work placement initiative in school-level programmes under the Ministry of Education, and a new adult apprenticeship initiative (Starter) under the MLWSS. There is, as yet, no co-ordinated governance system for vocational education and training, but the National Economic Council has taken steps to improve co-ordination within government (National Economic Council, 2016).

The education system of Israel

The basic education system is divided along ethnic and religious groups

One compulsory year of kindergarten is state-funded, and two further optional years of pre-schooling are for the most part state-funded. Compulsory schooling begins at grade 1 at age 6, with primary school from grades 1 to 6, intermediate school from grades 7-9 and secondary school in grades 10-12. Primary and secondary schools are divided into four systems, secular Jewish, religious Jewish, "ultra-orthodox" (Haredi), and Arab (Arabic speaking) (Wolff, 2017).

Attainment of basic skills is weak on average

The Programme for International Student Assessment (PISA) 2015 results for 15-year-olds show Israeli 15-year-olds scoring 15-20 points below the OECD average in the three domains of reading, maths and science. But beneath these average performances lie some of the largest variations in performance observed in any OECD country. For example, in mathematics, while performance at the level of the top decile is very similar to the OECD average (601 points compared with the OECD average of 605), Israeli performance at the lowest decile is 40 points weaker than the OECD average performance at the lowest decile (332 points compared with the OECD average of 373) (OECD, 2016a). This large spread in performance is primarily related to the different performance observed in the different educational sectors, with differences of the order of 100 points, in the domains of science, reading and mathematics, between the Hebrew-speaking and Arabic sectors (Jerusalem Post, 2016). The measurement of performance in the Haredi sector remains problematic, as most Haredi institutions for boys apparently do not take part in the PISA test (Gruber, 2017).

The majority of upper-secondary students enter the general academic track

Around 60% of upper-secondary students enrol in general academic upper-secondary education, one-third choose one of three 'technological' tracks at this level under the Ministry of Education, while only 3% enrol in MLWSS industrial schools or apprenticeship pathways (ETF, 2014). While 90% of 18-year-olds complete upper-secondary education, around half obtain the *Bagrut* matriculation qualification that provides access to higher education (66% if retakers up to the age of 18 are included) (Handjipanayiotou, 2015). Among those with a Bagrut examination, 56% obtain 4-5 points in English and 20% obtain 4-5 points in mathematics, the level required in many university programmes (Ministry of Education, 2017a). As with the PISA results, these averages mask very large differences between social groups: only one in ten Haredi 18-year-olds obtain the *Bagrut*, just under half of their Arab-speaking counterparts, but nearly three-quarters of Hebrew-speaking (other than Haredi) 18-year-olds (OECD, 2016b).

Tertiary graduation rates have increased sharply and this increase has been driven by growth in non-university higher education institutions

Almost half (49%) of Israel's adult population aged 25-64 have tertiary qualifications, well above the OECD average of 35%, and the third highest rate of all OECD countries. Most have a bachelor's degree (OECD, 2017). Among those aged 31-34 (when most students have completed their studies) the proportion of first and higher degree holders has almost doubled, going from 22% to 40% between 1995 and 2011. While the number of students in universities has barely increased, academic colleges have grown from almost nowhere in the early 1990s to become the largest component of the higher education system, with around 100 000 students enrolled. Academic colleges provide undergraduate degrees more focused on professional training, they do not have Ph.D. programmes and are spread widely throughout the country, allowing more students to live at home while studying (Fuchs, 2015; Wolff, 2017). In 2013/14 there were 37 academic colleges (of which 16 non-publicly funded), and 21 academic colleges of education (teacher-training colleges). Within the college sector the non-publicly funded colleges have grown particularly fast, so that this sector alone accounted for around 20% of all students by 2012/13 (Council for Higher Education, 2014).

In other countries enrolment in non-university higher education programmes has also been growing

The academic colleges may be compared with the *Fachhochschulen* in German-speaking countries, Junior colleges in Korea, university colleges in the Nordic countries, and the HBO institutions in the Netherlands, all higher education institutions separated from universities, and with more emphasis on professional education and training than research. Often, as in Israel, recent increase in tertiary participation has been driven by growth in this sector. In Austria for example, graduation rates in tertiary-type A (corresponding to bachelor qualifications and above) have nearly trebled, rising from 10% to 29% between 1995 and 2009, with much of the growth attributable to the rapid development of *Fachhochschulen*, which provide bachelors and masters-level qualifications. Just over 40% of the 350 programmes were in technology and engineering in 2010/11; one-third in economic sciences; 14% in health sciences (Musset et al., 2013). Compared to the large tertiary system including both universities and academic colleges, Israel maintains a relatively small sector of short post-secondary vocational programmes.

Compulsory military service is an important feature of the school-to-work transition

Men serve in the Israeli Defence Force for just under three years from the age of 18, and women for two years, with exemptions for Arabs and ultra-orthodox Jews. In the Israeli Defence Force, many people learn skills applicable in civilian life, and through a new initiative, these skills are now being certified and recognised (National Economic Council, 2016). On exiting the military, young adults receive career guidance and a financial contribution that may be used for subsequent training and education. One effect of military service is that many Jewish Israelis enter university or other training in their mid-twenties, and are relatively late in entering the labour market. The average age of Jewish students in their first year of tertiary academic study was 24.5 in 2011 (Fuchs, 2015).

Israel's vocational education and training system

At upper-secondary level VET has declined over the last half century

In the 1960s and 70s around 60% of the cohort pursued vocational programmes at upper-secondary level, leaving upper-secondary academic studies in gymnasia to a small elite. During this period VET was expanded to cater to students who were considered not suitable for academic studies. Many students channelled into VET programmes come from the Sephardim communities from North Africa and the Middle East who migrated to Israel in the 1950s and 60s (Taub Center, 2015). In response to the criticism that the system perpetuated socio-economic inequality across ethnic groups and did not match the rising skills demands, the occupation-specific content was reduced in most VET programmes and the name changed into 'technological education'. Over the last half century the proportion of students in VET has fallen dramatically.

One-third of upper-secondary students study in technological tracks

Currently, just over one-third of students in upper-secondary education, under the Ministry of Education, study in 'technological' tracks. Hereafter, these students will be called 'technological students' and programmes they are in 'technological programmes'. Out of these students, around 37% study in higher status fields related to engineering (e.g. in electronics, computer, software engineering or bio-tech) designed for students who excel academically. Another 37% follow 'middle level programmes' related to computers, ICT, media and advertising catering to students with an average academic achievement and preparing for technician and practical engineering programmes. And finally 'lower level' programmes preparing for professions such as health, hospitality, business administration and pedagogy enrol 25% of technological students, mainly those from the bottom fifth of the distribution of academic achievement (Shavit, 2013). These three tracks all prepare pupils for the *Bagrut* exams, though with different success rates (Blank, Shavit, Yaish, 2015). In an attempt to reduce difference between the three tracks (engineering, technical and professional) the Ministry of Education has been reforming technological education and does not distinguish between the three groups any more (Ministry of Education, 2017b).

In addition, a small proportion of upper-secondary students pursue apprenticeships

A small proportion of upper-secondary students (about 3% or 11 600 students) undertake youth apprenticeship under the auspices of the MLWSS. Many are drop-outs from mainstream education, and on that basis, they are permitted to enter apprenticeships (given a general legal requirement for classroom education). These are provided on a dual model with the schools seeking out work placements in industry. Around 25% of the schools which offer apprenticeships are linked to a company or a military base. Students pursue just 14 credits of the *Bagrut*, of which half are in technical subjects; the remaining 7 general subjects will include Hebrew, Maths and English. These 14 units are sufficient to enter a short-cycle post-secondary practical engineering programme, but not university. In the 9th and 10th grades there is more academic study, and students start their work placement in 11th grade. In school, they split between academic studies and workshop time 50/50. Their vocational certification at the end of the programme is, for example, in a subject like mechanics, with a sub-specialism in earthmoving.

Independent networks of schools play a large role

Most vocational training for young people is delivered through not-for-profit school networks, of which Общество Ремесленного Труда or "Association for Vocational

Crafts" (ORT) is the largest – often they run both academic and vocational schools. Networks providing training to adults are typically for-profit (see Box 1.2).

> **Box 1.2. The school networks in Israel**
>
> Networks of VET providers, independent from government, manage many of the schools. 40% of vocational students are enrolled in schools managed by the two largest networks - ORT and *Amal* (the Hebrew word for labour). Both these networks are prominently engaged with the ministries in discussions about arrangements for the governance, management and reform of VET. The network of schools managed by ORT includes 100 000 students and 7 500 staff in 200 upper-secondary schools, industrial schools, educational centres, and technical, engineering and academic colleges in 55 municipalities across Israel. The AMAL educational network manages 128 educational institutions including high schools, junior high schools and colleges and with a total enrolment of over 40 000 students. AMAL emphasises technology, the sciences and the arts for all strata of the population from high-achieving young people of Israel's elite to young people who are at risk. Both networks place emphasis on innovation in developing new approaches to teaching and learning in the schools that they manage.
>
> *Source:* ETF (European Training Foundation) (2014), *Mapping Vocational Education and Training Governance in Israel*, www.etf.europa.eu/web.nsf/pages/GEMM_Mapping_VET_governance_Israel.

Practical engineering and technician programmes are offered at post-secondary level

Most students in these programmes are under the auspices of the MLWSS (for those undertaking the programmes as adults) with a small minority under the Ministry of Education (for those pursuing the programmes immediately following school) (MOITAL, 2012). Practical engineering is a post-secondary short-cycle programme of 2 years full-time and 3 years part-time. The programme includes a variety of technical subjects, including mechanics, civil engineering, etc. Technician programmes last one year. Most MLWSS students are in their twenties, having completed military service. 47% of them are working (and therefore study part-time in the evening). They normally require a partial *Bagrut* to enter the programme; alternatively, they may pursue a preparatory programme to bring them up to the right level of skills in maths, English and Hebrew. Practical engineering and technician programmes, provided in 60 technical colleges across the country, lead to national exams and a national qualification. 28 out of the 60 colleges cater to ultra-orthodox men and women. In 2016 there were 23 318 students in practical engineering and 1 748 in technician programmes. The unit price of teaching a practical engineering programme per full-time student year is around one-third of the cost of university programmes, a point addressed in Chapter 3. A potential weak point of practical engineering is the limited engagement of employers – although they are to some extent involved in the final project required to graduate. This is a challenge for those studying full-time, who are not already working in a related field.

Occupational certification is managed by MLWSS

Occupational certifications are administered by MLWSS in more than 100 different professions on the basis of examinations. There are 211 basic certifications, and 76 upgraded ones. Some 70 000 people each year take these examinations, sometimes at the end of an educational programme, and sometimes as a stand-alone examination. The main limitation of this system is that employer engagement is weak (OECD, 2014).

The Ministry of Education runs a separate system of professional certifications

The Ministry of Education runs a separate system of certifications that are delivered to students in technological programmes. It includes nine levels of performance and certifies occupational skills and academic performance. This certification has been introduced recently and replaced the previous one that had a low value on the labour market and in the society (Ministry of Education, 2017b). The majority of certifications delivered so far were in the field of administration.

Programmes for adults

Israel has programmes specifically designed for adults that lead to professional certifications awarded by the MLWSS. These include courses organised and funded by the Ministry and private courses funded by individuals but preparing for a formal qualification. Training to adults can also be provided by other ministries (see Table 1.1). Main programmes for adults include: On-the-job training (OJT), Class in the Workplace and the New Starter programme. OJT affords employers the opportunity to hire new workers as regular employees and train them in the workplace through a designated mentor, according to the demands of their job. Employers are eligible to receive two types of assistance from the MLWSS: partial funding of the employee's pay during the training period and partial funding of the mentor's pay. The training is for up to 3 months (with some extensions possible). There is no final examination. In 2015 just over 1 700 workers received OJT (Ben Rabi et al., forthcoming). A Class in the Workplace allows employers to offer specialised courses for groups of job seekers in professions in high demand. The practical segment of the training takes place at the workplace, while the theoretical studies are held by the employer or at an accredited VET institution. The employers receive funding for the course and a grant for placing workers with special incentives from priority population groups. Courses last 650 hours on average. Quite small numbers are involved – there were only 132 trainees in 2016 The Starter programme has been recently launched as a pilot. (Ben Rabi et al., forthcoming).

Table 1.1. Participation of different ministries in training

Ministry	Duration	Number of programmes	Number of students (2015 or latest available)
Health	7.5 months to 2.5 years	6	233
Aliyah and Integration	3 to 10 months	4+	100
Defence	6 to 10 months	3	85
National Infrastructures, Energy and Water Resources	18 to 2 700 hours	8	602
Tourism	450 to 600 hours	3	558

Source: Adapted from King, J. (2017), *The Involvement of Five Ministries in Training for the Labour Market*, prepared by Myers-JDC-Brookdale Institute at the request of the Ministry of Labour, Social Affairs and Social Services (unpublished).

Curricula, inspection and quality assurance are handled by the two main ministries

National examinations and assessments, the curriculum and text books, and the school inspection system are organised in parallel by the Ministry of Education and the MLWSS. The school networks and local authorities also play a significant role at the practical level of quality assurance. The Ministry of Education maintains sectoral committees, including the social partners, academic representatives, and other relevant ministries and representatives of teachers from the field. Each committee has a responsibility for quality assurance and the curriculum in their respective field. Two inspectorates, one for the Ministry of Education and one for MLWSS, ensure that standards are set and adhered to in the schools (ETF, 2014).

Policy development

New initiatives aim to develop work-based learning

Two new initiatives seek to extend the use of work-based learning in the vocational system (Ben Rabi et al., forthcoming). The first programme is for adults and the second for youth. They are examined in more depth in Chapter 2.

- Under the MLWSS, a new initiative is seeking to develop adult apprenticeships through the 'Starter' programme. This programme is still in a pilot phase, with only a few hundred students, and evaluation is under way. The programme offers courses of 6-9 months with apprentice time divided about equally between the workplace and the classroom. While the period of study is much shorter, in principle the qualifications obtained are the same as could be obtained in youth apprenticeship. Employers are enthusiastic about this programme and the Ministry aims to expand it.

- Under the Ministry of Education, technological students will have an opportunity to carry out short work placement with employers. In 2017 8 892 technological track students in 173 schools participated in this programme (Ministry of Education, 2017b). The students are unpaid, but the participating employers can receive incentive payments from the Ministry of Education.

A new government-backed report by an inter-ministerial group is likely to have a significant impact

As a means of encouraging more co-ordination in the system, the government established an inter-ministerial group to look at VET and agree on ways of improving co-ordination. Their report (National Economic Council, 2016) notes the inefficiency of currently fragmented arrangements, and recommends:

- The creation of a national qualifications framework to cover all aspects of education and training.

- Enhanced pathways for mobility within and between the different education tracks in Israel.

- New ways of recognising professional experience in adults so that they can obtain a high school completion certificate.

- An increased proportion of ultra-Orthodox and Arab students enrolled in advanced technological and vocational studies.

- Better integration and recognition of training in the Israeli Defence Force with academic, professional and vocational qualifications.
- More integration of practical engineering and technician programmes within a system of lifelong learning, to include strengthened links with the technological tracks in schools and on into higher education.

Implementing the recommendations of the National Economic Council will require continuing efforts

These commendable recommendations are a significant step forward, and implementation would be very helpful. They do leave a challenge since their implementation would require involvement of different parts of government. Recommendations of this nature, which cut across the responsibilities of different ministries, can easily lose momentum in the absence of a single focal point with appropriate powers and clear responsibility. The report of the National Economic Council will therefore need to be actively followed up to ensure that implementation takes place. This OECD review will therefore make proposals for a body to take forward the implementation of these recommendations (see Chapter 4).

Assessment: Strengths and challenges

The importance of VET is now widely recognised

Israel's key strength includes measures taken in response to the pressing demands on its skills system. There is now a wide recognition of the importance of vocational education and training in Israel, with new initiatives by the MLWSS, the Ministry of Education and across government through the report of the National Economic Council.

A sequence of initiatives address many of the key challenges

The importance of work-based learning has been well recognised in the commitment of the two main ministries to develop apprenticeship and work-based learning both at upper-secondary level and among adults. A strong economy and consequent skills shortages create the opportunity to pilot innovative new approaches, such as the 'Starter' programme, and obtain employer support, as employers are under pressure to explore new approaches to skills development. While numbers are small, some of the piloted models, and individual employer-level initiatives, appear to be of good quality. Professional evaluations are in place for these pilots, and the results of the evaluations should help to guide policy development. Data protection arrangements allow student data to be linked to administrative data, so the potential to drive policy with solid outcome evidence is there. The issue of how to integrate the skills learnt in military service with civilian life is also being addressed in a new scheme.

Building on these initiatives a step change is needed to develop VET

While all of these developments are steps in the right direction, they do not go far enough. It is not clear that they have gained sufficient momentum to ensure that they are self-sustaining. Building on these initiatives, now is the time to make a step change in the Israeli vocational education and training system, so that it can gain the prominence it deserves in the face of skills bottlenecks in the economy, and the economic marginalisation of some social groups.

Relative to other OECD countries few students in Israel pursue VET paths

Upper-secondary education in Israel does not, for the most part, seek to prepare young people for particular jobs or careers. A very small minority pursue apprenticeship-type upper-secondary education. At post-secondary level, again, practical engineering and technician programmes serve only a small proportion of the cohort with short-cycle post-secondary vocational qualifications. This contrasts with other OECD countries, where 20-30% of young people sometimes have short post-secondary qualifications (OECD, 2014). If alternative pathways prepare well for the entry to labour market and successful careers the size of the VET system is not a concern. However if these pathways prepare poorly for the labour market, an expansion of good quality VET could be envisaged.

Initial VET serves two connected objectives

If Israel provides less vocational education and training (at upper-secondary and post-secondary level) to young people than other countries, one question is whether this is because of less need for these types of vocational skills. Very broadly, initial vocational education and training in OECD countries serves two connected purposes. The first is to meet the labour market need for a wide range of technical, trade, craft and professional skills, particularly in areas where a university education is not a necessity. The second is to help those who do not pursue, for one reason or another, the classical route from general academic education to university, to succeed in the world of work. This function is profoundly important, and some countries with strong vocational education and training systems, especially apprenticeship, have been particularly effective in securing smooth transitions from school to work for the vast majority of young people (OECD, 2010b).

VET is a tool to increase productivity in some sectors

In Israel, productivity is low in manufacturing industries that sell to the domestic market and in non-tradable industries. (Bank of Israel, 2016) notes that sectors with low productivity rely on non-complex and low technology work methods. This is consistent with findings from the Survey for Adult Skills showing that Israelis employed in semi-skilled sectors (e.g. clerks, service and shop workers, craft and related trade workers, plant and machine operators) are less likely to solve problems, use computers and other technologies than their counterparts in many other countries (see Figure 1.1). By contrast, labour productivity in the electronics industry in Israel is higher than the OECD average. (Bank of Israel, 2016) concludes that productivity improvements in underperforming sectors depend on improvements in worker's proficiency and the quality of education in Israel. A more effective VET system, targets on areas of skills deficiency, might help to meet this challenge.

There are skills shortages in many sectors

By international standards Israel has relatively many jobs requiring high- level skills and relatively few elementary low- skilled occupations, as classified by ISCO. While this shows that the Israeli economy is particularly dependent on the supply of highly skilled labour, labour shortages are observed in many sectors and occupations. (Central Bureau Statistics, 2017) shows that in 2016, labour shortages were most acute in professional jobs (including the sector of science and engineering professionals, health professionals, and IT technology professionals), and in jobs of skilled workers such as in manufacturing and construction. While professional jobs typically require some type of post-secondary education, in many countries education and training for skilled worker occupations is provided at secondary level.

Figure 1.1. Use of computers by blue-collar workers

16-65 year-olds reporting using computers on their jobs

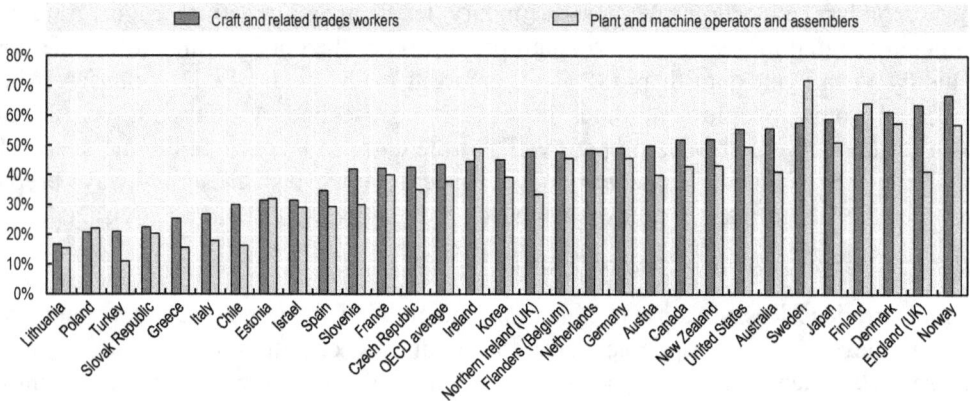

Source: OECD calculations based on OECD (2018b), *OECD Survey of Adult Skills (PIAAC)* (Database 2012, 2015), www.oecd.org/site/piaac/publicdataandanalysis.htm.

StatLink http://dx.doi.org/10.1787/888933734778

A key challenge for Israel is to meet the needs of those with few skills and qualifications

In terms of social cohesion, there are relatively few options for those who do not obtain the *Bagrut* examination. There are also more specific concerns: a long-standing anxiety about low rates of economic activity among ultra-orthodox (Haredi) men and Arab women has eased slightly in the last few years, but the challenge of targeting vocational training on these two groups in a way that will transition them into work remains significant.

Policy options

Weak supply and strong demand for vocational skills implies the need for a co-ordinated strategic reform of vocational education and training in Israel. This major challenge underpins the more specific proposals advanced in the chapters which follow.

Chapter 2: Developing work-based learning

Chapter 2 argues that the development of VET in Israel could be significantly aided through attention to work-based learning, building on a range of current initiatives to develop apprenticeship and work-based learning both for young people and adults. International evidence shows that work-based learning has multiple benefits, but in Israel technological education, enrolling the majority of upper-secondary VET students, has few tangible labour market returns. Reforms are needed to integrate apprenticeship and work-based learning as a routine part of upper-secondary vocational education and training rather than an option for potential drop-outs. For adults, diverse work-based learning measures, including apprenticeship may help to alleviate skills shortages and help to integrate disadvantaged social groups into the labour market.

Policy options include:

- To improve outcomes from initial VET, Israel should expand and develop the work-based learning component of VET programmes. This would involve an expansion of apprenticeship programmes, and development of systematic work-based learning placements in selected technological programmes.

- Currently apprenticeship is designed as a path for drop-outs and is seen as a low status option. To become an attractive option both to young people and employer it should be fully integrated into the mainstream upper-secondary system. This means that the requirement of a special exemption to enter an apprenticeship should be dropped.

- To expand apprenticeship programmes for adults Israel should devise incentive and support measures based on analysis of relevant costs and benefits for different target groups (e.g. by gender, ethnic and religious minorities, age) as the individual costs and benefits can vary.

Chapter 3: Involving employers through youth apprenticeship and sectoral training levies

Chapter 3 argues that an active engagement of employers is a critical precondition for the development and expansion of vocational programmes, including programmes with work-based learning, in Israel. While the involvement of all the stakeholders – public authorities, participants and employers – in the design and provision of work-based learning programmes is a key strength of these programmes, realising this strength is very demanding. Successful involvement of the different stakeholders requires the reconciliation of different interests. Adjustment in the design of apprenticeships in Israel can create stronger incentives for employers to offer apprenticeship training. Sectoral training levies may help to increase an overall amount of training and address skills shortages in some sectors.

Three policy options are:

- Expand youth apprenticeships on prestigious occupations, including in public administration, to attract able students to the programme, as discussed in Chapter 2. Support employers in the provision of high-quality apprenticeships by providing services such as mentoring, training for apprentice instructors, help with administrative tasks, and support to employers working with disadvantaged youth.

- Israel may review its wage setting in line with arrangements encountered in other countries to ensure apprenticeship is beneficial to employers. If this is implemented Israel may analyse the impact of lower wages on individual participation and if necessary, provide additional financial support to apprentices.

- Low productivity and skills shortages in several economic sectors are holding back Israel's economic growth. While employers would collectively benefit from more workforce training, it is not always in the individual interest of an employer to offer training. To overcome this barrier, and create the step change necessary to improve the supply of skills, Israel may wish to support the establishment of sectoral training levies initiated by social partners (employers and trade unions), which have been used successfully in some European countries.

Chapter 4: Creating a coherent and transparent vocational education and training system

Chapter 4 argues that the Israeli vocational system is relatively fragmented. To drive reform, improve coherence and transparency, and meet Israel's need for vocational technical skills, Israel should establish an overarching steering body for Israel's vocational education and training system. This body might be called the National Council for Vocational Education and Training. The National Council should be established on a statutory basis, with its composition and responsibilities set out in law, so as to ensure its authority. It should have its own budget and secretariat. The Council should include representatives of employers, trade unions, government (including from the Ministry of Education and the MLWSS), vocational training institutions, minority groups and wider society. The main responsibility of the National Council would be to guide the development of the vocational education and training system.

To this end the National Council should:

- Publish a strategic (5-10 year) plan for the development and expansion of vocational education and training in Israel. This plan would be based on an assessment of emerging skills demands, and analysis of how those skills needs are to be met, and the steps which need to be taken by different ministries to meet those demands.

- Ensure that the different programmes and initiatives within the VET sector are evaluated, and publish an annual report, reporting on the contribution of the different elements of the VET system to the longer-term objectives, and making policy recommendations.

- Take direct charge of quality assurance and inspection of vocational provision, replacing the (duplicated and uncoordinated) separate arrangements currently in place. The National Council should also take responsibility for evaluating the quality of the system, and undertake research to this end, reporting this in its annual report.

- Take forward the recommendations of the report of the National Economic Council, guiding the development of a set of information tools to make the vocational system transparent to its users. Such tools would include relevant aspects of a national qualifications framework and strengthened outcome data.

In Israel many young people fail to obtain the *Bagrut* and many do not enter higher education. The offer for these young people is currently weak and inequality is higher. Israel's economic performance, and social cohesion depends on giving these young people relevant working skills and integrating them into the labour market. Israel may consider expanding and diversifying provision at post-secondary level, and promote pathways so that vocational choices are not dead ends.

This implies action at three levels:

- The offer of short post-secondary vocational programmes needs to be diversified and expanded, and funded on the same basis as higher education in the interests of both efficiency and fairness.

- A strengthened institutional foundation should be established by promoting much fuller co-operation between the technical and academic colleges, and in some cases mergers. This co-operation should be used to diversify the offer of one and two-year post-secondary vocational programmes beyond the current technical areas.

- To secure the status of post-secondary vocational programmes, and to meet skill needs, these programmes need to sustain the option of subsequent progression to higher education.

Chapter 5: Improving literacy and numeracy in VET programmes

Chapter 5 shows that weak literacy and numeracy – poor basic skills - are more common among Israeli adults than in most other OECD countries. Graduates of initial VET (as their highest qualification) often have weak basic skills. These skills gaps significantly weaken workforce skills, and are a barrier to labour market integration for disadvantaged groups. While effective education provided early on is the best long-term response, strengthened attention to literacy and numeracy development is required in vocational programmes, including apprenticeships, technological education and programmes for adults.

Policy options include:

- In Israel a large share of young people leave initial VET with poor basic skills. Often, the low basic skills of VET graduates will reflect weaknesses in the entrant population to these programmes. But there is also some evidence pointing to low quality teaching leading to modest skills acquisition in some programmes. Israel should therefore invest in initial VET to ensure adequate levels of literacy and numeracy in all students, identifying the weakest performers and targeting teaching resources on them to improve performance. This means exploring different teaching approaches, including teaching literacy and numeracy in the context of apprenticeship and technological education.

- There are multiple skills shortages in the adult workforce in Israel, and the basic skills of the adult population are relatively weak, particularly for some social groups. To tackle this challenge, Israel should build basic skills education systematically into adult programmes and military service, while also ensuring that effective programmes are in place for those groups that are exempt from military service.

- Basic skills are particularly low among Arab Israelis and Haredi Jews. These populations are also less likely to participate in the labour market and are more at risk of living in poverty. Since basic skills are closely related to the labour market outcomes and life chances addressing basis skills weaknesses in these populations should be a priority.

References

Bank of Israel (2016), *Bank of Israel - Press Release - Excerpt from the Fiscal Survey and Collection of Research Issues: Basic Skills of Workers in Israel and Industry Productivity*, Bank of Israel, www.boi.org.il/en/NewsAndPublications/PressReleases/Pages/19-07-2016.aspx.

Ben Rabi, D. et al. (forthcoming), *Apprenticeship and Work-Based Learning in Israel. Background Report for Israel Project: Aiming High – Review of Apprenticeship*.

Blank, C., Shavit, Y. and M. Yaish (2015), "Tracking and attainment in Israeli secondary education", in Chernichovsky, D. and A. Weiss (eds.), *State of the Nation Report 2015. Society, Economy and Policy in Israel*, Taub Center for Social Policy Studies in Israel, Jerusalem, http://taubcenter.org.il/singer-series-state-nation-report-2015/.

Central Bureau of Statistics (2017), *Supply and Demand in the Labour Market in Israel in October-December 2016 and Summer of 2016. Press Release*, www.cbs.gov.il/www/hodaot2017n/20_17_095e.pdf.

Council for Higher Education (2014), *The Higher Education System in Israel 2014*, http://che.org.il/wp-content/uploads/2012/05/HIGHER-EDUCATION-BOOKLET.pdf.

ETF (European Training Foundation) (2014), *Mapping Vocational Education and Training Governance in Israel*, www.etf.europa.eu/web.nsf/pages/GEMM_Mapping_VET_governance_Israel.

Fuchs, H. (2015), "The socioeconomic situation of young adults in Israel", in Chernichovsky, D. and A. Weiss (eds.), *State of the Nation Report 2015*, Taub Center for Social Policy Studies in Israel, Jerusalem, http://taubcenter.org.il/wp-content/files_mf/snr2015fullreport.pdf.

Gruber, N. (2017), *Why Israel Does Poorly in the PISA Exams – Perceptions Versus Reality*, Shoresh Research Paper, http://shoresh.institute/research-paper-eng-Gruber-PISA.pdf.

Handjipanayiotou, P. (2015), "More Israeli students pass bagrut exam, but success rate still low", *Education News*, 25 July 2015, www.educationnews.org/international-uk/more-israeli-students-pass-bagrut-exam-but-success-rate-still-low/.

Jerusalem Post (2016), "Israeli students lagging behind OECD counterparts", *Jerusalem Post*, 6 December 2016, www.jpost.com/Israel-News/Israeli-students-lagging-behind-OECD-counterparts-474572.

King J. (2017), *The Involvement of Five Ministries in Training for the Labour Market*, prepared by Myers-JDC-Brookdale Institute at the request of the Ministry of Labour, Social Affairs and Social Services (unpublished).

Ministry of Education Israel (2017a), *Shkifut (transparency) report. Data from the School Year 2015-2016*, http://ic.education.gov.il/QvAJAXZfc/opendoc_pc.htm?document=shkifut.qvw&host=qvsprodlb&sheet=SH02.

Ministry of Education (2017b), *Programs in Technological and Vocational Education in Israel – October 2017 – Summary for the OECD*.

Ministry of Industry Trade and Labour (MOITAL) (2012), *Vocational Education and Training (VET): Background Report for Israel, OECD Project: Skills Beyond School*, Ministry of Industry, Trade and Labour, The Manpower Training and Development Bureau, Israel.

Musset, P., M. Kuczera and S. Field (2014), *A Skills beyond School Review of Israel*, OECD Reviews of Vocational Education and Training, OECD Publishing, Paris, http://dx.doi.org/10.1787/9789264210769-en.

National Economic Council (2016), וההשכלה ההכשרה מערכות בין והניעות האקרדיטציה מערך לשיפור משרדי בין צוות *(Inter-ministerial Team Report to Improve the System of Accreditation and Mobility between the Education and Training Systems)*, www.pmo.gov.il/BranchesAndUnits/direcgeneral/Pages/Accreditation.aspx.

OECD (2018a), *OECD Economic Surveys: Israel 2018*, OECD Publishing, Paris, http://dx.doi.org/10.1787/eco_surveys-isr-2018-en.

OECD (2018b), *OECD Survey of Adult Skills (PIAAC)* (Database 2012, 2015), www.oecd.org/site/piaac/publicdataandanalysis.htm.

OECD (2017), *Education at a Glance 2017: OECD Indicators*, OECD Publishing, Paris, http://dx.doi.org/10.1787/eag-2017-en.

OECD (2016a), "Annex B1.5 Results (tables): Mathematics performance among 15-year-olds", *PISA 2015 Results (Volume I): Excellence and Equity in Education*, PISA, OECD Publishing, Paris, http://dx.doi.org/10.1787/9789264266490-en.

OECD (2016b), *Education Policy Outlook: Israel*, OECD, Paris, www.oecd.org/israel/Education-Policy-Outlook-Country-Profile-Israel.pdf.

OECD (2014), *Skills beyond School: The Synthesis Report*, OECD Reviews of Vocational Education and Training, OECD Publishing, Paris, http://dx.doi.org/10.1787/9789264214682-en.

OECD (2010a), *OECD Reviews of Labour Market and Social Policies: Israel*, OECD Publishing, Paris, http://dx.doi.org/10.1787/9789264079267-en.

OECD (2010b), *Learning for Jobs*, OECD Reviews of Vocational Education and Training, OECD Publishing, Paris, http://dx.doi.org/10.1787/9789264087460-en.

Wolff, L. (2017), "Education in Israel: Divided society, divided schools", *Moment*, Washington, DC, www.momentmag.com/education-in-israel-divided-schools-divided-society/.

Chapter 2. **Developing work-based learning in Israel**

Chapter 2 argues that the development of vocational education and training (VET) in Israel could be significantly aided through attention to work-based learning, building on a range of current initiatives to develop apprenticeship and work-based learning both for young people and adults. This would involve an expansion of apprenticeship programmes and development of systematic shorter work-based learning placements in selected school-based VET programmes. Currently apprenticeship is designed as a path for dropouts and is seen as a low status option. To become an attractive option both to young people and employers it should be fully integrated into the mainstream upper-secondary system. For adults, diverse work-based learning measures, including apprenticeship, may help to alleviate skills shortages and better integrate disadvantaged social groups into the labour market.

The statistical data for Israel are supplied by and under the responsibility of the relevant Israeli authorities. The use of such data by the OECD is without prejudice to the status of the Golan Heights, East Jerusalem and Israeli settlements in the West Bank under the terms of international law.

Introduction: Building work-based learning in different contexts

Work-based learning (WBL) can help to meet some major challenges faced by Israel

As explained in Chapter 1, Israel faces major challenges both in providing the skills needed by a growing economy and in integrating more disadvantaged Israelis into the labour market. This chapter argues that VET can help to address these challenges but at present the VET system is weak relative to the scale of these challenges. This chapter first discusses different examples of work-based learning across OECD countries and in Israel. Second, it argues that the current VET system in Israel can be strengthened through a more effective use of apprenticeships and expansion of work placements in technological programmes.

VET and work-based learning in other countries

Work-based learning plays a key role in many VET programmes

WBL is an integral part of apprenticeship programmes, so that, for example in Switzerland a student cannot start an apprenticeship programme unless he or she secures a work-based placement with an employer. Sometimes WBL is a mandatory part of a programme based in schools or colleges. At the other extreme, some VET programmes are heavily concentrated in schools and colleges, with practical elements delivered in school workshops, and work-based learning being an optional and sometimes minor element.

WBL in apprenticeship and some other programmes can be highly structured

Work-based learning is learning through participation in, and/or observation of work, commonly in the workplace and under the supervision of an employer. It includes diverse activities, ranging from short work placements with employers provided to school students at one end of the spectrum, to programmes, including apprenticeship, involving extensive training on employer premises. Apprenticeship and some other vocational programmes with mandatory components of work-based learning typically lead to a recognised qualification, and involve a structured mix of:

- work placement with an employer that leads to the development of new skills, and that can involve productive work and,
- off-the-job education and training at school, college or other educational and training provider involving no or limited productive work.

The sequencing of on and off-the-job training varies between apprenticeship systems

Extensive work-based learning is at the core of apprenticeship programmes, where working with employers typically represents at least 50% of the programme duration. The time-sequencing of on and off-the-job education and training varies between different apprenticeship systems – sometimes involving one or two days a week in a school or college as in most 'dual system' apprenticeships, but sometimes in larger time chunks for the off-the-job component, for example in Canada and Ireland. In some cases a full apprenticeship is preceded by a pre-apprenticeship programme, which can involve general education, as well as, quite often, work placements. Such programmes can target disadvantaged youths who would not be able to complete an apprenticeship without targeted preparation. Denmark, Germany, the Netherlands, Norway, Switzerland are among countries with strong apprenticeship systems, while England (United Kingdom) is currently going through an ambitious reform that should lead to a significant expansion of apprenticeships, including the development of degree apprenticeships in partnership with universities.

In some countries with large apprenticeship system most apprentices are young

Some apprenticeship systems serve primarily to transition young people from school to work. In Switzerland for example, in 2014/15 three-quarters (76%) of apprentices were under 20 (Mühlemann, 2016). But other countries have a more even mix of adult and youth apprentices, with some of the adults already having significant work experience. In Germany in 2014 around 56% of apprentices were under 20, and a further 20% were between 21 and 23 years old, the older apprentices being a mix of those who complete the academic upper-secondary *Abitur* before entering apprenticeship, and others who have often spent some time in pre-apprenticeship programmes. In Australia in 2016, apprentices and trainees under 20 and those aged 20-25 represented 34% and 43% of all apprentices and trainees respectively (Australian Bureau of Statistics, 2016). In 2010 and 2011, 20 year-olds and older represented more than 50% of all apprentices in Finland (Stenstrom and Virolainen, 2014).

Table 2.1. The duration of apprenticeship programmes and how apprentices spend their time

	Duration of the programme including off-the-job period and work placement with the company	Time allocation in apprenticeship programmes	Workplace time spent in productive and non–productive tasks
Austria	3-4 years	66% - work place 20% - off-the-job education and training 14% - leave and sick days	83% of the time with the company is spent on productive work
Denmark	3.5-4 years (typically)	Missing	Missing
England, UK	Min. 12 months - average around 15 months	At least 20% in off-the-job education and training	
Germany	Mostly 3 years	56% - work place 29% - off-the-job education and training 14% - leave and sick days	77% of the time with the company is spent on productive work
Israel	3-4 years	Work-based learning is provided in the last two years, 1-3 days per week	Missing
Netherlands	2-4 years		
Norway	Mostly 4 years (Shorter programmes are available for disadvantaged students)	Typically, first two years are spent in school and the last two with the company	1 year of training 1 year of productive work
Sweden	3 years	Apprentices spend as much time in school as in a work place with the company	Missing
Switzerland	3-4 years (2-year programmes in some occupations leading a lower level qualification)	59% - work place 27% - off-the-job education and training 14% - leave and sick days	83% of the time with the company is spent on productive work

Source: Kuczera, M. (2017), "Striking the right balance: Costs and benefits of apprenticeship", *OECD Education Working Papers,* No. 153, http://dx.doi.org/10.1787/995fff01-en.

Outside apprenticeship, WBL assumes different forms

Some common models of WBL include:

- Some school and college-based VET programmes may include work placements with employers but typically not exceeding 50% of the programme duration. For example, in Finland a work placement of at least 6 months is mandatory in upper-secondary vocational programmes, and represents about 20% of the programme duration (Finnish National Board of Education, 2016).

- Work placements at post-secondary level sometimes require students to carry out projects with employers on a specific topic. For example in Denmark, such placements occupy a minimum of three months in two-year professional programmes, and a minimum of six months in three year professional bachelor programmes (Field et. al., 2012).

- Some more informal forms of work-based learning do not provide a full preparation for a specific occupation, but instead are intended to allow students to explore future career options, familiarise themselves with the work environment and acquire some work relevant experience. For example, in the United States students follows or "shadow" the employee as normal work activities are performed over the course of a working day (Kuczera, 2011).

Different forms of WBL may target different age groups

Many countries have different programmes with shorter and longer work placements, sometimes reflecting the needs of different learner groups. In the Netherlands, there are two vocational routes at upper-secondary level: apprenticeships with on-the-job time representing nearly 70% of the programme duration on average, and school-based vocational programmes with mandatory work placements representing around 30% of the programme duration. Both paths may lead to the similar vocational qualification, but the school-based option is more popular with younger students. 73% of students in this programme are under 20, compared with 30% in the apprenticeship route (Fazekas and Litjens, 2014; Christoffels, Cuppen, and Vrielink, 2016). Similarly, in Finland vocational programmes in schools with shorter work placements are more popular among young people, while apprenticeships serve older students with some work experience.

VET and work-based learning in Israel

Technological programmes under the MoE now occasionally involve WBL

Recently a component of work-based learning was introduced in technological programmes, but it remains optional. It provides students with an opportunity of observing the real work during visits to employers. In this respect technological education and training in Israel is similar to some other countries such as Czech Republic, Italy and Korea where work placements in school-based VET programmes are not mandatory. In Israel, the government provides a subsidy to employers offering these short work placements.

There are also apprenticeships for young people

In 2016, about 3% of upper-secondary (high school) students in Israel (11 600) studied in apprenticeship programmes lasting four years (grades 9-12), under the responsibility of the Ministry of Labour, Welfare and Social Services (MLWSS). In apprenticeship, education and training in the first two grades is provided solely in school while in grades 11 and 12 students alternate education in school with training in companies. Depending on the profession, students spend 1 to 3 days per week in the work placement (Ben Rabi et al., forthcoming). Apprenticeships are mainly provided to disadvantaged students. To help them successfully complete the programme they are provided with targeted support and assistance.

WBL is increasingly an element in technician and practical engineering programmes

There have also been efforts to develop work-based learning at post-secondary level in technician and practical engineer programmes. As the team was informed during the study visit some students in engineering programmes carry out a final project with industry during the last four months of the programme. To encourage the involvement of employers, and so provision of work placements to students, a council for certified practical engineers and technicians was created (Pur and Littig, 2017). This initiative is in line with conclusions of the previous OECD study Skills beyond School that recommended establishment of a national body involving all the key stakeholders, including employers and unions, to provide strategic guidance on the development of the VET system (Musset, Field and Kuczera, 2014).

Table 2.2. Vocational programmes for adults involving work-based learning

	Target population	State funding to employers	State funding to individuals	Duration	Contract and apprentice salary	Content and qualifications
Class in Workplace	- The person cannot be employed by the employer at the beginning of the course. In practice participants are unemployed or job seekers; - For a course to open an employer or a group of employers should recruit at least ten participants (although this varies depending on the profession)	- The employer gets the cost of the course reimbursed: 75% during the course and 25% conditional on the employing at least 1/3 of participants. If the theoretical part takes place in a college the government transfers funds to the college. - Additional grant for employing graduates from disadvantaged groups	- Since courses are paid by the state they are free of charge to individuals; - Subsistence allowance of NIS 1 500 (around EUR 350) per month; - Grant upon successful completion and receiving a certificate	4-12 months depending on the sector and profession	- There is no contract between the employer and the participant; - Participants do not receive pay during the programme?	- Includes practical (40-60%) and theoretical training (in a workplace or a college); - Content is defined by the Ministry of Labour in collaboration with the employer; - Upon passing an examination, participants receive a certificate delivered by the Ministry of Labour
Starter	- Targeted at unemployed, job seekers and low-paid workers who are at least 18-year-olds; - Provided in sectors with skills shortages; - For a course to open an employer or a group should recruit around 20 participants	- One-off payment of NIK 5 400 (EUR 1 254) towards the wage of the mentor and the apprentices; - Grant of NIK 1 500 for every participant who passes the exam	Theoretical training in a college is paid by the Ministry; - Participants are eligible for travel expenses and receive a stipend during the first stage of the programme (NIK 1 500 per month, with the total amount not exceeding NIS 6 000)	6-9 months	- The programme management signs a contract with the employer, and a separate contract with the college; - The apprentice signs a commitment. - The apprentice receives a wage in the 2nd stage of the training while in the work place. The wage should be above the min wage (NIK 5 000) and he/she receives social benefits	- Stage 1 (6-8 weeks): theoretical and practical studies at a college -Stage2 (4-7 months): participants alternate 3 days a week in the college and 3 days in the work place; - Certificates are delivered by the Ministry of Labour; - Curriculum is planned by the Ministry in collaboration with the employer

Source: Ben Rabi D. et al. (forthcoming), *Apprenticeship and Work-Based Learning in Israel. Background Report for Israel Project for Israel Project: Aiming High – Review of Apprenticeship*; National Insurance Institute of Israel (n.d.), "General Information - Minimum Wage", www.btl.gov.il/English%20Homepage/Mediniyut/GeneralInformation/Pages/MinimumWage.aspx (accessed 12 September 2017).

Several programmes for adults involve WBL

Some of the programmes for adults involve substantial work experience. This chapter discusses two of these programmes: Class in the Workplace and Starter. Hereafter these programmes are called work-based learning/apprenticeship programmes for adults. The Starter has been launched recently as a pilot with 214 individuals participating. First evaluations are positive and there are plans to expand it. A separate 'on-the-job training' programme, targeting mainly unemployed people and job seekers, will not be discussed as it does not lead to a formal qualification and does not include off-the-job education and training. For more details on this programme see (Ben Rabi et al., forthcoming). Class in the Workplace and Starter remain very small. Details of Class in Workplace and the Starter are provided in Table 2.2.

Policy options: Developing work-based learning for young people and adults

Work-based learning in programmes for young people

The current school-based VET system, enrolling the majority of VET students, serves some students well by providing them with strong academic skills and preparing them well for entry to university. But others are left behind. These are students who do not pass matriculation exams (*Bagrut*), who drop out during the course, and who do not continue to higher levels of education for other reasons. These young people are currently very poorly equipped for entry to the labour market or for further study. International experience shows that students with this profile could benefit from strong VET programmes with substantial components of work-based learning.

- To improve outcomes from initial VET, Israel should expand and develop the work-based learning component of VET programmes. This would involve an expansion of apprenticeship programmes, and development of systematic shorter work-based learning placements in selected technological programmes.

- Currently apprenticeship is designed as a path for drop-outs and is seen as a low status option. To become an attractive option both to young people and employer it should be fully integrated into the mainstream upper-secondary system. This means that the requirement of a special exemption to enter an apprenticeship should be dropped.

Work-based learning in programmes for adults

The labour market in Israel is tight, with few jobseekers and many vacancies. Poor basic skills (as discussed in Chapter 5), and an initial VET system with limited focus on labour market needs, further exacerbate skills shortages. Apprenticeship programmes for adults, offering both occupation-specific skills and basic (generic) competences, could help to alleviate the problem.

- To expand apprenticeship programmes for adults Israel should devise incentive and support measures based on analysis of relevant costs and benefits for different target groups (e.g. by gender, ethnic and religious minorities, age) as the individual costs and benefits can vary.

Policy arguments: The rationale for reform

Several arguments support the policy options set out above, proposing an orchestrated strengthening of work-based learning in vocational programmes for young people and adults. First, there is a very wide range of evidence from other countries on the diverse benefits of work-based learning. Second, the labour market returns from most strands of technological education – which in most cases do not involve work-based learning – are weak, contrasting with international evidence showing good returns to vocational programmes involving work-based learning. Third, the current organisation of work-based learning in Israel, particularly in respect of young people, tend to stigmatise it as an option of last resort. Fourth, to resolve this last challenge and for wider reasons, apprenticeships for young people need to be properly integrated into the education and training system as a whole. Fifth, apprenticeship programmes for adults need to be further developed, taking account of how the costs and benefits of participation bear on different potential target groups. These five arguments are detailed below.

Policy argument 1. International evidence suggests multiple benefits from work-based learning

WBL yields a diverse range of benefits

Work placements have been widely recognised as an effective means of equipping people with generic and job relevant skills by combining learning and work, as summarised in (OECD, 2010).

- Workplaces provide a strong learning environment because they allow students to acquire practical skills on up-to-date equipment and under trainers familiar with the most recent working methods and technologies. Rapidly changing technologies mean that equipment quickly becomes obsolete and VET institutions are often unable to afford modern equipment. Workplace training will therefore often be more cost-effective, since it makes use of equipment already available in firms.

- In the workplace, students develop key soft skills, such as dealing with customers, work discipline, teamwork, problem-solving skills etc. Much evidence indicates the growing labour market importance of soft skills (Deming, 2015), and suggests that many soft skills are more effectively learnt in workplaces than in classrooms (OECD, 2010).

- WBL improves school-to-work transition. There is some evidence that VET graduates who have experienced more WBL (such as apprentices) have stronger labour market outcomes, in terms of duration of search, unemployment spells and wages, than those who choose another type of upper-secondary education (Bratberg and Nilsen, 1998; van der Klaauw et al., 2004; European Commission, 2013). Overall, countries with a high share of youth in apprenticeships have lower rates of disconnected youth and youth experiencing a difficult transition to employment (Quintini and Manfredi, 2009). First labour market experiences have lasting consequences, and youth unemployment has long-term 'scarring' effects with high costs for both individuals and society (Bell and Blanchflower, 2011; Nilsen and Reiso, 2011).

- WBL ensures VET provision matches labour market needs. Employer willingness to offer work-based learning is an indicator of their support for the associated vocational programme. Employers can influence the number and mix of places in VET through their willingness to offer workplace training – for example in apprenticeships. Even short work placements can serve to signal the skills needs of employers. VET colleges and schools, cannot immediately respond to rapidly changing demand, as new equipment is costly, teachers and trainers cannot be easily changed or retrained, and programmes take some time to complete. This means that the mix of provision tends to be biased towards the training that schools and colleges can easily provide. Programmes which are more reliant on WBL can therefore be more responsive to changing employer demand.

- WBL yields both useful work for the employer, and a means of recruitment. Students who undertake useful work generate a productive benefit for the employer (see Schweri et al., 2003; Mühlemann, 2016; Kuczera, 2017). Employers taking apprentices can observe the performance of the apprentices and recruit the best from among them. Unlike school-based VET, apprenticeships are therefore automatically linked to labour market needs and the placements can serve to signal the skills needs of employers. In Israel, apprenticeship is provided in half of the schools under the responsibility of the MLWSS for the Arab population and all the schools linked to industries.

Policy argument 2. Outcomes from upper-secondary VET are good for some Israeli students, but others are left far behind

15-year-old students in Israel have strong preferences for skilled occupations

Upper-secondary VET typically prepares young people for semi-skilled occupations. The Programme for International Student Assessment (PISA) 2015 data show that in all countries 15-year-olds say that they would prefer to work in skilled rather than in semi-skilled jobs. But these preferences vary across countries. In Israel 90% of young people aspire to jobs requiring high-level skills, more than other countries participating in the survey with the exception of Mexico, and fewer young people than elsewhere wish to work in semi-skilled occupations. Despite these aspirations, 40% of upper-secondary students enrol in VET programmes. Possible explanations for this difference between preferences and subsequent enrolment include:

- In Israel, unlike other countries, the more demanding upper-secondary VET tracks prepare young people for skilled occupations.

- Some forms of upper-secondary VET in Israel lead to jobs with low pay and poor career prospects and are therefore seen as undesirable by parents and students. But academic selection forces many students to enter these less demanding VET programmes.

- Israeli 15-year-olds have unrealistic aspirations, which are subsequently brought into line with reality through academic selection into VET tracks.

All these explanations may apply in part, perhaps to different sub-tracks of upper-secondary VET students. Better understanding of the labour market outcomes from the different sub-tracks of upper-secondary VET would help to identify the explanations that apply, and possible policy responses.

Figure 2.1. In Israel, more young people aspire to skilled jobs than in most other countries

2015 PISA, % of 15-year-olds by desired occupation

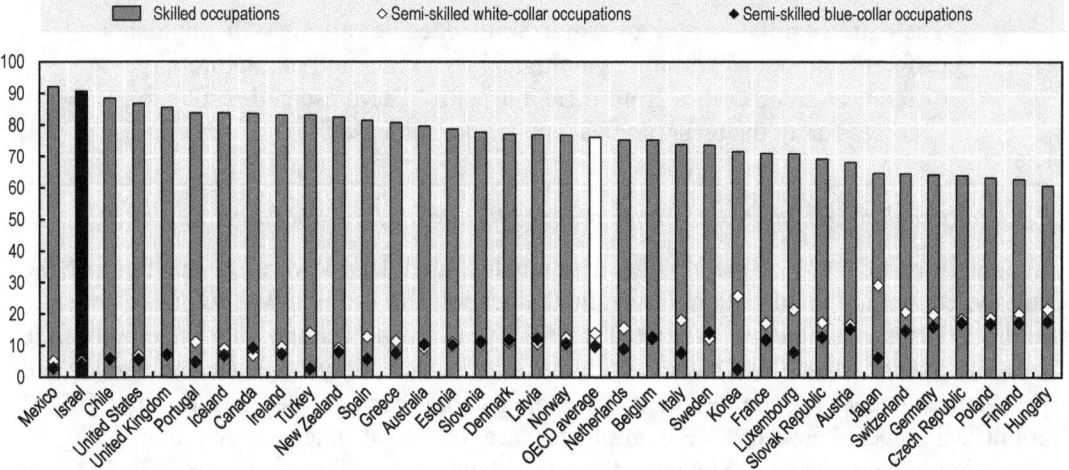

Note: See ILO, 2012, International Standard Classification of Occupations. Structure Group definitions and correspondence tables, ISCO-08, ILO, Geneva. In this report occupations were grouped in four categories: Skilled occupations such as professionals, managers, technicians and associate professionals, which typically require post-secondary education and training including post-secondary vocational and longer academic degrees; white-collar semi-skilled occupations, including clerical support and sales workers, typically requiring lower or upper-secondary education and occasionally shorter post-secondary vocational qualifications; blue-collar semi-skilled occupations, with education and skills requirements similar to the previous category above; and elementary occupations relying on skills corresponding with primary education.
Source: OECD, *PISA 2015 Database*, www.oecd.org/pisa/data/2015database/.

StatLink ⟶ http://dx.doi.org/10.1787/888933734797

In Israel nearly all upper-secondary VET students are in technological education

Given that apprenticeship in Israel is currently small in scale, and technological education under the Ministry of Education enrols the overwhelming majority of upper-secondary VET students, the measured outcomes from upper-secondary VET mainly reflect outcomes from technological education (see Box 2.1). The discussion on outcomes which follows will also take into account differences in students' ability, preferences and life circumstances, and how the current system addresses these diverse needs.

Box 2.1. Analysis of outcomes from upper-secondary VET in Israel, with the Survey of Adult Skills

The analysis which follows draws on data from the OECD's Survey of Adult Skills, which measures the skills of individuals and provides information on a range of background characteristics.

Upper-secondary VET qualifications refer to qualifications identified by countries as vocational. In Israel upper-secondary VET designates technological qualifications (with or without matriculation). Upper-secondary VET graduates are those who graduated from technological education, and for whom upper-secondary VET is the highest

> qualification. The Survey of Adult Skills data does not allow to identify those who completed a higher-level qualification on the top of upper-secondary VET.
>
> The data from the Survey of Adult Skills does not allow to distinguish different sub-tracks within technological education and to capture large differences in outcomes from different paths. The presented results are averages for all the technological sub-tracks combined.

Technological programmes sometimes prepare for higher levels of education

In Israel around 16% of technological graduates aged 16-40 were, at the time of the survey, continuing in education. Given that education and training was reformed in Israel in the 1990s, the sample was restricted to 16-40 year-olds to capture only the effect of the current system. Most (90%) were studying at post-secondary level (in technician and practical engineer programmes, or those ending with a bachelor degree). In other OECD countries, upper-secondary VET graduates are the most likely to be continuing in education in New Zealand, Slovenia, the Netherlands and Chile (see Figure 2.3). In Chile and Slovenia the majority of those in education study in post-secondary programmes while in New Zealand, the Netherlands and Australia around one-third enrol in other upper-secondary programmes.

Figure 2.2. Share of upper-secondary VET graduates enrolled in education

16-40-year-olds with upper-secondary VET as the highest qualification. In Israel upper-secondary VET refers to technological education

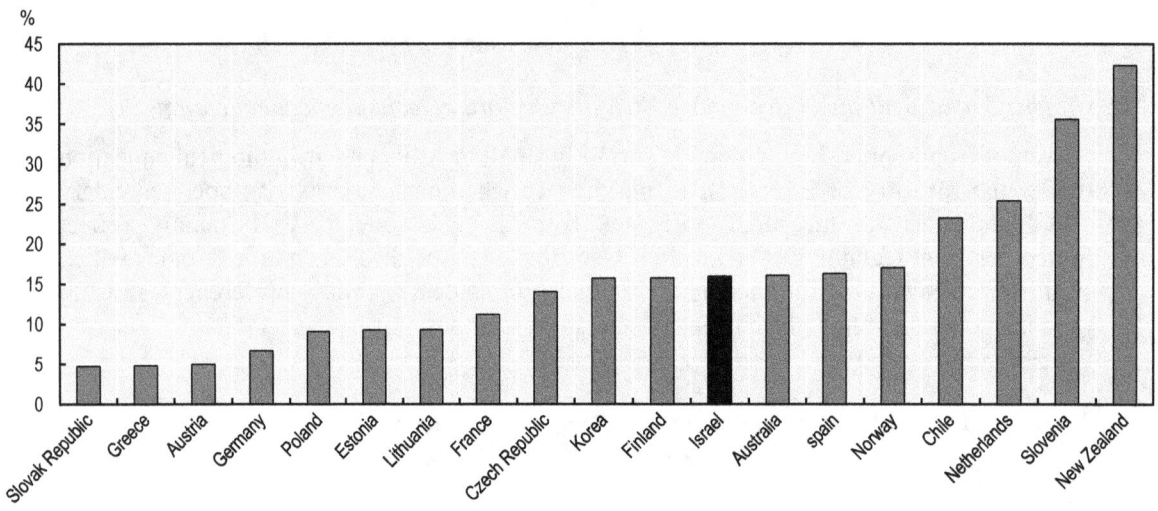

Note: Results are presented only for countries with a sufficient number of observations, and where VET can be distinguished from academic programmes.
Source: OECD calculations based on *OECD Survey of Adult Skills (PIAAC)* (Database 2012, 2015), www.oecd.org/site/piaac/publicdataandanalysis.htm.

StatLink http://dx.doi.org/10.1787/888933734816

Technological education on its own has limited labour market benefits

In Israel, the wages of technological graduates (with or without matriculation) do not differ from wages of individuals with similar characteristics (age, gender and parental education) but with lower (below upper-secondary) qualifications (see Figure 2.3). These findings contrast with those from countries where apprenticeship accounts for a large proportion of VET (Austria, Germany, the Netherlands and Norway) and where VET yields a large wage premium. Kuczera (2017) shows that, in these countries, apprentice graduates realise a significant wage premium relative to similar adults (in terms of individual characteristics, numeracy skills, and the company size) but with education below upper-secondary level, and even in comparison with those with academic upper-secondary qualifications.

Figure 2.3. In Israel, there is limited evidence for a wage premium from technological education

16-40-year-olds. Percentage wage advantage for graduates of upper-secondary VET relative to those qualification levels below upper-secondary. In Israel upper-secondary VET refers to technological education.

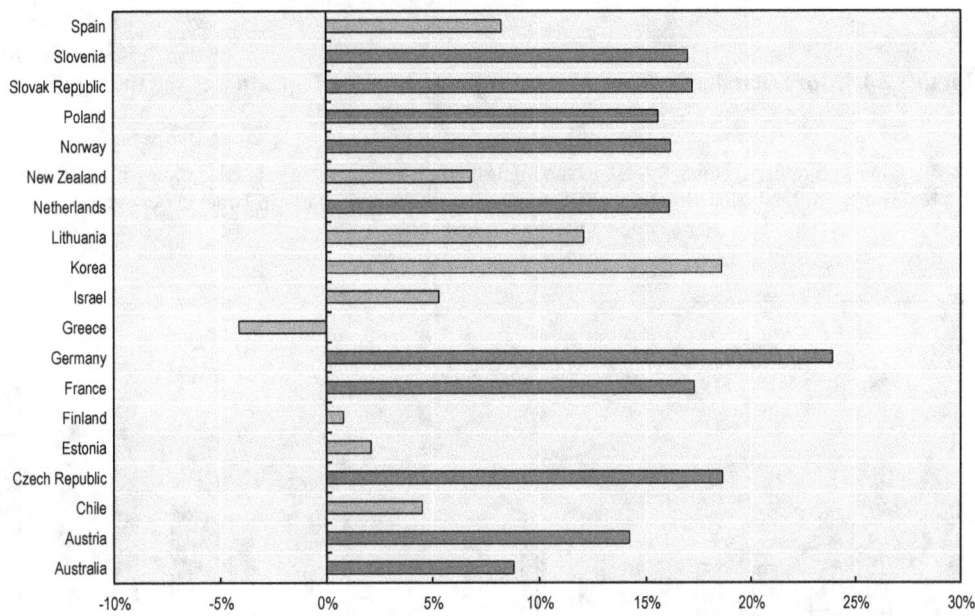

Note: Coefficients from the ordinary least squares (OLS) regression of log hourly earnings. Coefficients adjusted for age, gender and parental education. Wage outliers were dropped, namely wages above the 99th percentile and wages below the 1st percentile. Results statistically significant (at 5%) are marked in darker tone. Results are presented only for countries with a sufficient number of observations, and where VET can be distinguished from academic programmes. Those still in education are excluded from the analysis of the labour market outcomes as they are often in part-time and unqualified jobs. The analysis was performed in the age group 16-40. Given that many young Israelis are in the army a similar analysis was run among those aged 21-40 year-olds. The results of the two analyses were consistent and lead to similar conclusions. Adding as a control variable performance on numeracy and the number of employees working for the employer diminishes the effect of the VET qualification on wages in most countries. This shows that VET graduates are more likely to work for larger employers and have better numeracy skills than those without upper-secondary qualifications. With PIAAC data it is unfortunately impossible to say whether better numeracy skills result from the quality of teaching in VET programmes or reflect the fact that entrants to VET paths have stronger basic skills than those not continuing in education.
Source: OECD calculations based on OECD *Survey of Adult Skills (PIAAC)* (Database 2012, 2015), www.oecd.org/site/piaac/publicdataandanalysis.htm.

StatLink http://dx.doi.org/10.1787/888933734835

Many technological graduates perceive their jobs as unqualified

In Israel, one in five technological graduates (and not in education) work in skilled and semi-skilled jobs (by ISCO classification). In comparison to many other countries, graduates from technological programme are less likely to work in elementary occupations in principle requiring no or low-level qualifications. Despite this, 60% consider their jobs as 'unqualified' (they report that no formal education or education below upper-secondary is needed to get their current job) more than in many other countries (see Figure 2.4). This might mean that Israelis are just more pessimistic about their jobs. But it may also reflect less demanding work content for some jobs in Israel, in comparison with nominally similar jobs in other countries. This last possibility would be consistent with an observed gap between labour productivity in Israel and OECD countries on average, and across sectors in Israel. In summary, technological graduates on average, more often than their counterparts in some other countries, work in jobs they see as 'unqualified', and do not realise any wage advantage from their technological qualification. This outcome may be because technological graduates lack higher-level skills, or because, despite good skills, they are trapped in jobs reliant only on low-level skills.

Figure 2.4. More than half of Israel's upper-secondary VET graduates see their job as unqualified

16-40-year-olds with upper-secondary VET as the highest qualification and not in education who report being in jobs requiring no formal education or qualification below upper-secondary. In Israel upper-secondary VET refers to technological education.

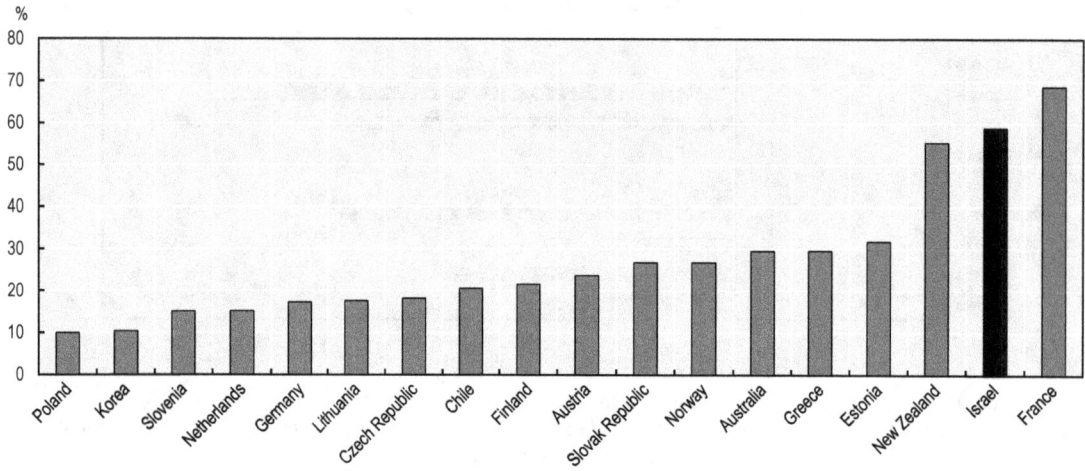

Source: OECD calculations based on OECD *Survey of Adult Skills (PIAAC)* (Database 2012, 2015, variable D_Q12a), www.oecd.org/site/piaac/publicdataandanalysis.htm.

StatLink http://dx.doi.org/10.1787/888933734854

There are large differences in outcomes from three technological paths

Studies which distinguish between different technological paths show that there are large differences in outcomes across the three major technological tracks. A recent study shows that graduates from engineering sub-tracks earn 17% more and those from the lowest sub-tracks earn 12% less, than those who graduated from academic upper-secondary paths.

Graduates from the 'middle level' sub-tracks of technological education have similar earnings as the comparison group (Ministry of Finance, forthcoming).

Some students are not well-served by the current system

Currently, around 40% of upper-secondary students enrol in technological education and youth apprenticeships, and 60% in academic programmes (Taub Center, 2015). In 2014, 53% of the age cohort (17-18 year-olds) passed the matriculation exam required to study at university (Lewis, 2015). These are students who are likely to continue in education at higher levels later on. But Ministry of Finance (forthcoming) shows that the pass rate in the matriculation exam ranges from 75% in engineering paths to 40% in lower sub-tracks of technological education. These variations are due not only to differences in academic achievement and socio-economic background in the different student groups, as could be expected, but also to differences in the intensity and quality of academic preparation that takes place within these programmes (Taub Center, 2015).

Drop-out rates are substantial

Over 40% of teenagers in Israel say that they feel alienated from school and nearly one-third are often absent from school (Skop, 2014). In 2012, 22 257 students dropped out at some point during secondary education (grade 7-12), representing 3% of the student population in the relevant grades. Around 30% of those who dropped out enrolled in alternative education such as yeshiva schools and apprenticeships run by the MLWSS. The highest drop-out rates were in Haredi and Arab communities, and among recent migrants (Salansky and Portnoy, 2013).

These findings suggest that strengthened WBL could help VET students realise better outcomes

In summary, the current upper-secondary VET system, particularly in the more demanding technological sub-tracks, serves some students well by providing them with strong academic skills, allowing them to continue to university and leading to well paid jobs. But other students do not pass matriculation exams, drop out during the course of studies and do not continue to higher education for other reasons. These students are poorly equipped for further education, they often work in jobs which they perceive as requiring no qualifications, and for wages no greater than those available to unqualified workers. This is both wasteful and damaging to social inclusion. Given international evidence that strong VET programmes, particularly those involving apprenticeship, can offer rewarding careers to graduates, there are good grounds for Israel to build on its current VET system through an emphasis on apprenticeship, work-based learning and basic skills, as a means of serving the economy, improving productivity, and integrating young people into the labour market.

Policy argument 3. Apprenticeship is too often seen in Israel as an option of last resort

In Israel, youth apprenticeship is designed as a path for drop-outs

Access to apprenticeships at upper-secondary level, administered by the MLWSS, is currently limited to students who have dropped out from schools supervised by the Ministry of Education, or are at risk of dropping out and have received an exemption from attending the regular education system. This inevitably stigmatises apprenticeship in the eyes of both students and employers.

In other countries, apprenticeship can be high status

In other countries some apprenticeship programmes can be very demanding in terms of academic requirements. For example, in Switzerland, of top performers on PISA, 25% enter the most demanding apprenticeship programmes leading to the professions of electronics engineer, commercial employee, optometrist and medical laboratory technicians (Swiss Coordination Centre for Research in Education, 2014, p.119). At the same time in Switzerland, alongside regular apprenticeships lasting 3 to 4 years, shorter, two-year apprenticeship programmes are available to students who did not secure a regular apprenticeship or were at risk of dropping out (Swiss Coordination Centre for Research in Education, 2014, p.148). Since 2002 students who successfully complete two-year apprenticeship have received a certificate that enables them to continue in education and training. Evaluations show that graduates from certified two-year programmes have better labour market prospects than those who have completed an uncertified apprenticeship (Kammermann et al., 2011) This shows that within an apprenticeship system in Switzerland that is chosen by many of the brightest, it remains possible to include effective options for those who struggle. This might be a model for the development of apprenticeship in Israel (see also Kis, 2016).

Policy argument 4. Apprenticeships for young people need to be better connected with other parts of the upper-secondary education and training system

Apprenticeships are now better integrated with other parts of the education and training system in Israel

Apprentices who complete their studies but do not pass all their exams, are now entitled to a 12-year school completion diploma, bringing their treatment into line with other students in the Ministry of Education system. The diploma is required to enter post-secondary programmes and is recognised on the labour market (Ben Rabi et al., forthcoming). Israel should now build on this positive step by offering apprentices a fuller opportunity of passing matriculation exams, a key means of attracting more able students, who commonly will aspire to further and higher education. Currently, only 3% of apprentices take a partial matriculation exam (Ben Rabi et al., forthcoming). Interviews conducted during the review visits suggest that most apprentices are not academically prepared to succeed at it. Also, apprentices do not receive "protective score" from the MoE when taking the matriculation exams, so that the final grade is determined only by the external exam, and not based on the previous achievement and school evaluation, which is the case for the students in the Ministry of Education.

Stronger pathways from upper-secondary VET to post-secondary education are vital

Creating workable pathways between upper-secondary VET and post-secondary options would improve the image of VET and provide a quality option for those who are less academically oriented. This would, as discussed in Chapter 4, include diversification of post-secondary non-university programmes in sectors such as health, childcare, services, that would allow technological and apprenticeship graduates to continue to higher levels of education.

Policy argument 5. Programmes for adults could help to address skills shortages but currently they reach too few individuals

WBL programmes for adults could play a key role in integrating disadvantaged social groups

WBL programmes for adults, offering both occupation-specific skills and basic (generic) competences, could help to alleviate skills shortages. These programmes should focus on activating adults who are outside the labour force, upskilling those who are in low-skilled employment and re-training those in occupations where employment is expected to shrink. Such measures might also be applied, in targeted ways, to engage the social groups that currently have low rates of economic activity – particularly Haredi men and Arab women.

Adults face several barriers to participation

Ben Rabi et al. (forthcoming) argue that attracting candidates to the programmes for adults is a major challenge, particularly in scaling up these initiatives. Thus:

- The cost of participation is often a barrier. While in Israel, many programmes are provided at no cost to individuals, participants incur opportunity costs - what they would earn had he/she not been in training. The opportunity cost is particularly high in the Class in the Workplace programme, as participants do not receive any wage during the programme. In the Starter programme participants should be paid at least the minimum wage, but the wage payment only begins in the second stage of the programmes and does not cover the off-the-job part. However, participants in these programmes can receive subsidies which diminish the opportunity cost.

- For older adults the returns from education and training are lower than for younger people, because older people have less time left on the labour market in which to recoup their investment in training through higher wages.

- Evidence from other countries shows that particularly adults with lower education and lower basic skills, are sometimes not motivated to take part in training (Mühlemann, 2017).

- Finally, (Ben Rabi et al., forthcoming) argues that the low status of VET overall contributes to low adult participation in programmes for adults.

Many countries have measures supporting adult apprentices

Apprenticeship in Germany and Switzerland has traditionally been focused on young people. But in recent years both countries have begun to encourage adult learners to pursue apprenticeships, with financial incentives and other support measures (see Box 2.2). In Israel, there are some financial incentives for adults who wish to upskill, including subsidies that compensate for lost earnings. In *Class in the Workplace*, participants are eligible for a subsidy of NIK 1 500 and a grant upon passing mid-term and final examinations. *Starter* participants receive NIK 1 500 in the first stage of programmes provided in a college (see Table 2.2). The subsidy amounts to only around one-third of the minimum wage, so for many the opportunity cost of participating in training may still be too high. Some other measures in Israel are designed to help participants to complete the programmes. They include an initial screening of candidates, monitoring participants performance during the course, and the introduction of soft-skills workshops at the beginning of the course (Ben Rabi et al., forthcoming).

> **Box 2.2. Incentive measures for adult apprentices**
>
> **Germany** has been promoting apprenticeship among young adults (aged 25-35) in response to skills shortages and insufficient young apprentices in some sectors. In Germany individuals may receive financial support for education expenses, travel, child care, tutoring, and subsistence during the training). To encourage completion, apprentices receive a grant upon passing mid-term and final examinations. The role of these incentives in the observed increase in the proportion of apprentices over 23 (from 3% in 1993 to 12% now) is unclear.
>
> In **Switzerland** initiatives supporting the development of adult apprenticeships are more recent (evidence). In 2016 around 8% of apprentices were older than 24. In Switzerland, adult apprentices earn around two-thirds of the unskilled worker wage, compared to one-fifth for younger apprentices. All individuals under 35 can apply for a scholarship of a maximum CHF 12 000 per year (equivalent to two and half median monthly wage of an unskilled worker). Under some circumstance they can also apply for social assistance. Additional financial assistance is available to those who are unemployed.
>
> In **Canada**, unlike Germany and Switzerland apprenticeship has traditionally been for adults. In Canada apprentices can receive up to CAD 4 000) (the minimum average hourly wage in Canada is CAD 11.43 per hour) during apprenticeship programme. The apprentice wage starts at around 50% of the skilled worker wage, which is higher than in Switzerland and Germany. A low completion rate is a challenge in Canada with less than half of all apprentices completing the programme within 11 years. The high drop-out rate may be related to the fact that apprenticeships last five years, increasing the difficulty of sustained engagement.
>
> *Source*: Mühlemann, S. (forthcoming), *Apprenticeship Training for Adults*.

References

Australian Bureau of Statistics (2016), "Education and work, Australia, May 2016, Table 20 in Education and Work data set", (accessed 21 September 2017), www.abs.gov.au/AUSSTATS/abs@.nsf/DetailsPage/6227.0May%202016?OpenDocument.

Ben Rabi, D. et al. (forthcoming), *Apprenticeship and Work-Based Learning in Israel. Background Report for Israel Project: Aiming High – Review of Apprenticeship*.

Bell, D. and D. Blanchflower (2011), "Young people and the Great Recession", *Oxford Review of Economic Policy*, Vol. 27/2, pp. 241-67, http://dx.doi.org/10.1093/oxrep/grr011.

Bratberg, E. and Ø. A. Nilsen (1998), "Transition from school to work: Search time and job duration", *IZA Discussion Paper*, No. 27, Institute for the Study of Labor (IZA), https://ideas.repec.org/p/iza/izadps/dp27.html.

Christoffels, I., J. Cuppen and S. Vrielink (2016), "Verzameling notities over de daling van de bbl en praktijkleren, Rapport - Rijksoverheid.nl", Rapport, ECBO, MOOZ, www.rijksoverheid.nl/documenten/rapporten/2016/10/18/verzameling-notities-over-de-daling-van-de-bbl-en-praktijkleren.

European Commission (2013), *The Effectiveness and Costs-Benefits of Apprenticeships: Results of the Quantitative Analysis*, European Commission, Brussels, http://ec.europa.eu/social/BlobServlet?docId=11352&langId=en.

Fazekas, M. and I. Litjens (2014), *A Skills beyond School Review of the Netherlands*, OECD Reviews of Vocational Education and Training, OECD Publishing, Paris, http://dx.doi.org/10.1787/9789264221840-en.

Field, S., et al. (2012), *A Skills beyond School Review of Denmark*, OECD Reviews of Vocational Education and Training, OECD Publishing, Paris, http://dx.doi.org/10.1787/9789264173668-en.

Finnish National Board of Education (2016), *Key Figures on Apprenticeship Training in Finland*, www.oph.fi/download/177964_Key_figures_on_apprenticeship_training_in_Finland.pdf.

Kammermann M., B. Stalder and A. Hättich (2011), "Two-year apprenticeships – a successful model of training?", *Journal of Vocational Education & Training*, Vol. 63/3, pp. 377-396, http://dx.doi.org/10.1080/13636820.2011.586130.

Kis, V. (2016), "Work-based learning for youth at risk: Getting employers on board", *OECD Education Working Papers*, No. 150, OECD Publishing, Paris, http://dx.doi.org/10.1787/5e122a91-en.

Kuczera, M. (2017), "Striking the right balance: Costs and benefits of apprenticeship", *OECD Education Working Papers*, No. 153, OECD Publishing, Paris, http://dx.doi.org/10.1787/995fff01-en.

Kuczera, M. (2011), *OECD Reviews of Vocational Education and Training: A Learning for Jobs Review of the United States, South Carolina 2011*, OECD Reviews of Vocational Education and Training, OECD Publishing, Paris, http://dx.doi.org/10.1787/9789264114012-en.

Lewis, A. (2015), "Just half of Israeli teens pass 2014 matriculation", *The Times of Israel*, 22 July 2015, www.timesofisrael.com/just-half-of-israeli-teens-pass-2015-matriculation/.

Ministry of Finance (forthcoming), *The Chief Economist Weekly Review*.

Mühlemann, S. (2016), "The Cost and Benefits of Work-based Learning", *OECD Education Working Papers*, No. 143, OECD Publishing, Paris, http://dx.doi.org/10.1787/5jlpl4s6g0zv-en.

Mühlemann S. (forthcoming), *Apprenticeship Training for Adults*.

National Insurance Institute of Israel (n.d.), "General Information - Minimum Wage", www.btl.gov.il/English%20Homepage/Mediniyut/GeneralInformation/Pages/MinimumWage.aspx (accessed 12 September 2017).

Nilsen, Ø. A. and K. Holm Reiso (2011), "Scarring effects of unemployment", *IZA Discussion Paper*, No. 6198, Institute for the Study of Labor (IZA), https://ideas.repec.org/p/iza/izadps/dp6198.html.

OECD (2018), *OECD Survey of Adult Skills (PIAAC)* (Database 2012, 2015), www.oecd.org/site/piaac/publicdataandanalysis.htm.

OECD (2010), *Learning for Jobs*, OECD Reviews of Vocational Education and Training, OECD Publishing, Paris, http://dx.doi.org/10.1787/9789264087460-en.

Pur, S. and P. Littig (2017), *Promoting Research and Innovation in Vocational Education and Training (VET) in Israel. Final Report on the German-Israeli VET Project 2014 – 2016*, www.na-bibb.de/fileadmin/user_upload/na-bibb.de/Dokumente/06_Metanavigation/01_Ueber_uns/05_Deutsch-Israelisches_Programm/VET_report_15.01.2017_FINAL.pdf.

Quintini, G. and T. Manfredi (2009), "Going separate ways? School-to-work transitions in the United States and Europe", *OECD Social, Employment and Migration Working Papers*, No. 90, OECD Publishing, Paris, http://dx.doi.org/10.1787/221717700447.

Salansky, M. and H. Portnoy (2013), *Computation of Dropout in Schools Supervised by the Ministry of Education during the School Year and in the Transition to the Following Year*, Central Bureau of Statistics, State of Israel, www.dst.dk/en/consulting/projects/Israel/ComponentB.

Schweri, J., et al. (2003), *Kosten und Nutzen der Lehrlingsausbildung aus der Sicht Schweizer Betriebe*, Chur/Zürich, Ruegger Verlag.

Skop, Y. (2014), "Over 40% of Israeli teens feel alienated from school", *Haaretz*, 16 July 2014, www.haaretz.com/israel-news/.premium-1.605340.

Stenstrom, M-L. and M. Virolainen (2014), *The Current State and Challenges of Vocational Education and Training in Finland, Nord-VET: The Future of VET in the Nordic Countries Report 1B Finland, Nord VET*, Roskilde University, Roskilde, (accessed 26 July 2017).

Swiss Coordination Centre for Research in Education (2014), *Swiss Education Report 2014*, Aarau, http://skbf-csre.ch/fileadmin/files/pdf/bildungsmonitoring/Swiss_Education_Report_2014.pdf.

Taub Center for Social Policy Studies in Israel (2015), *State of the Nation Report 2015. Society, Economy and Policy in Israel*, Jerusalem, http://taubcenter.org.il/wp-content/files_mf/snr2015fullreport.pdf.

van der Klaauw, B., A. van Vuuren and P. Berkhout (2004), "Labor market prospects, search intensity and the transition from college to work", *IZA Discussion Paper*, No. 1176, Institute for the Study of Labor (IZA), https://ideas.repec.org/p/iza/izadps/dp1176.html.

Chapter 3. A closer look at the economics of training in Israel: Involving employers through youth apprenticeship and sectoral training levies

> *Successful vocational education and training (VET) systems require strong employer involvement. This chapter explores how to make VET in Israel more attractive to employers. In Israel few employers are able to realise long-term benefits associated with recruitment of the most able apprentices, since many young apprentices enter the military service after the end of the programme. The chapter argues that a well-designed apprenticeship can be beneficial to employers even in the short term. To this end, Israel may support employers with providing high-quality training in workplaces. This includes measures such as helping employers with administrative tasks, training of apprentice instructors, and providing additional support to employers offering apprenticeships to disadvantaged youth. The chapter also discusses how to address some key skills shortages. Sectoral training levies initiated by social partners are one option.*

The statistical data for Israel are supplied by and under the responsibility of the relevant Israeli authorities. The use of such data by the OECD is without prejudice to the status of the Golan Heights, East Jerusalem and Israeli settlements in the West Bank under the terms of international law.

Introduction: How to engage employers?

An active engagement of employers is a critical precondition for the reform of vocational programmes in Israel. While the involvement of all the stakeholders - public authorities, participants and employers - in the design and provision of work-based learning programmes is a key strength of these programmes, realising this strength is very demanding. Successful involvement of the different stakeholders requires the reconciliation of different interests. This chapter explores two key issues – first, how to design apprenticeships in Israel so as to take account of the economic factors which drive employer engagement, and, second, the arguments how to address some key skills shortages with sectoral training levies being an option.

Employer engagement: An economic perspective

This chapter offers an economic perspective on the costs and benefits of work-based learning

An economic perspective on the costs and benefits of work-based learning provides a framework for the analysis of employers' behaviour, the conditions under which employers will want to provide work-based learning, and policy options that might further encourage its provision by employers. This analysis draws on findings from an evaluation of costs and benefits of apprenticeships carried out in Germany and Switzerland. This approach is then applied to Israel, taking full account of the different characteristics of Israel. It is applied to apprenticeships for young people under the responsibility of the Ministry of Labour, Welfare and Social Services (MLWSS) but also shorter work experience in school-based programmes (technological education) under the Ministry of Education and programmes for adults.

The economics of apprenticeship

Clearly, good apprenticeships, leading to good labour market outcomes for apprentices, require full employer involvement. Employers will normally provide apprenticeships when they believe that the benefits outweigh or are at least equal to the costs. The benefits emerge first, during the apprenticeship, through the productive contribution of apprentices, and second, after the end of the programme through recruitment of the most able apprentices, lower staff turnover and higher productivity. Employers can reap large benefits from this recruitment because labour markets are imperfect, and the full productive value of the graduate apprentice will therefore not be fully compensated in wages (e.g. Franz and Soskice, 1994).

Employers may be unaware of potential benefits

In countries where apprenticeship is less common, including Israel, employers may be more reluctant to invest in apprenticeships. While the costs of having apprentices are obvious, the benefits are less clear. Understanding those short and longer-term benefits and working out how best to realise them will take time. In Israel, an effective apprenticeship system should therefore not only lead to good benefits for employers, but also these benefits should be transparent to them.

Compulsory military service means that youth apprentices cannot usually be directly recruited as employees

In Israel, most young people serve in the army for 2-3 years after completing upper-secondary education. Employers providing training to these young people are therefore unable to recruit them immediately after the end of the apprenticeship programme, unless they are exempt from military service. While some apprenticeship graduates may eventually get back to the employer that provided their apprenticeship, many will change their careers or move to another employer. (Ben Rabi et al., forthcoming) argue that this factor discourages Israeli employers from engaging more fully in youth apprenticeship – it is just not that effective as a recruitment tool. So for Israeli employers to offer youth apprenticeship, they would normally have to see the return more immediately in terms of the work done by apprentices. An analysis of the costs and benefits of apprenticeship would help to estimate benefits accruing to employers in Israel in the current system. International experience shows that some apprenticeship systems can achieve this outcome through rapid training of apprentices, and by quickly using them in skilled roles, where the value of their contribution will be highest.

There is a risk apprentices are used solely as unskilled labour

All apprenticeship systems face the risk that apprentices might be exploited as unskilled labour. Using apprentices solely as unskilled labour requires little investment from employers but, if the apprentice wage is low, yields benefits associated with the productive unskilled work carried out by the apprentice. Simulations based on cost-benefit surveys show that Swiss employers could increase their net benefits by an average of EUR 22 000 per apprentice over the period of an apprenticeship if the apprentices performed only unskilled tasks while in the work place (Wolter and Ryan, 2011). Employers do not take advantage of this possibility in practice because apprenticeship regulations oblige employers to train – and this demonstrates the importance of such regulation. For example, in countries with strong apprenticeship systems (e.g. Switzerland and Norway) there is a curriculum defining skills apprentices should develop while in the work place (see for example curriculum for apprenticeship in electronics engineer in Switzerland (SEFRI, 2015).

Employers have to invest in training to be able to allocate apprentices to skilled tasks

Realising benefits from the skilled work of apprentices requires significant investment by the company (see Table 3.1). Apprentices need to be taught occupation-specific skills, which involves costs in terms of instruction time and equipment in addition to other costs.

Table 3.1. Costs and benefits associate with skilled and unskilled work of apprentices

	Apprentices contribute to unskilled work	Apprentices contribute to skilled work
Costs	Apprentice wage and other associated costs such as social security, etc.	Apprentice wage and other associated costs such as social security, etc.
	Administrative costs	Administrative costs
		Training equipment
		Wages of instructors/trainers
Benefits	Apprentice carry out productive work not requiring any additional training while in the workplace	Apprentice carry out productive work while in the workplace less time devoted to training

Source: Kuczera M. (2017), "Striking the right balance. Costs and benefits of apprenticeship", *Education Working Papers*, No. 153, http://dx.doi.org/10.1787/995fff01-en.

The Swiss model of apprenticeship has some relevance for Israel

The Swiss model is most relevant to Israel, given national service for men in Switzerland, and other features of the Swiss labour market which make it less likely that graduate apprentices will continue with the employer that provided them with apprenticeship training. Evidence from Switzerland shows that employers who invest in apprenticeship training can recoup their investment if they rapidly train up and allocate apprentices to skilled tasks, since the skilled tasks yield the most value to the employer. As an illustration of this point, a recent study has shown that apprenticeship in Austria yields lower benefits to employers than in Switzerland. This is because of higher apprentice wages (relative to skilled worker wages) in Austria than in Switzerland, and to the fact that Austrian apprentices spend less time in productive tasks than their Swiss counterparts (see Figure 3.1). It shows that in Switzerland apprentices by their second year spend roughly equal amount of their work place time in skilled and unskilled tasks. In Austria, apprentices only reach the same point in their third year. Although Austrian apprentices are less rapidly fully productive, Austrian employers have incentives to provide apprenticeship because of government subsidies and longer-term recruitment benefits (Moretti et al., 2017).

Figure 3.1. Allocation of apprentices to skilled and unskilled work in Switzerland and Austria

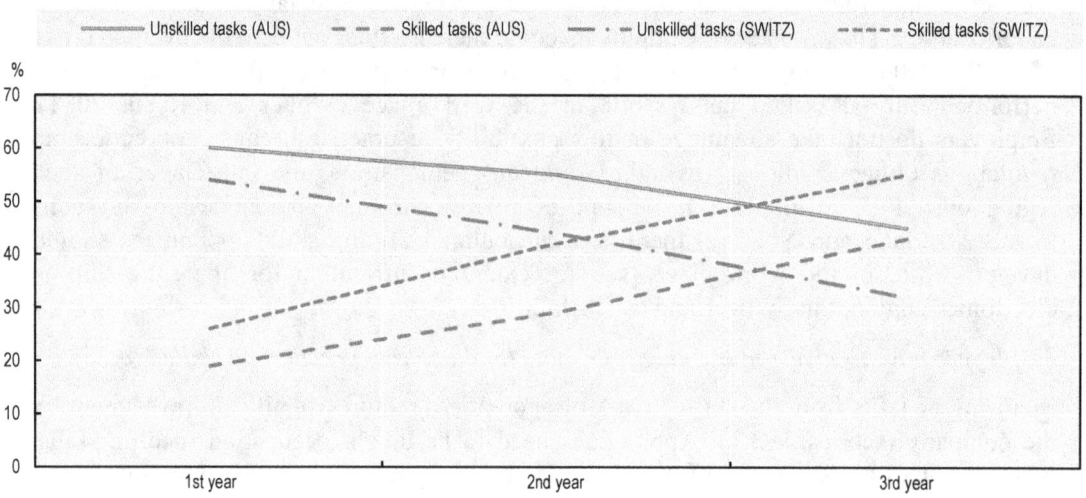

Source: Adapted from Moretti, et al., (2017), "So similar and yet so different: A comparative analysis of a firm's cost and benefits of apprenticeship training in Austria and Switzerland.", *IZA Discussion Paper*, No. 11081, https://econpapers.repec.org/paper/izaizadps/dp11081.htm.

StatLink http://dx.doi.org/10.1787/888933734873

Policy option 3.1: Making apprenticeships attractive to employers

Apprenticeship yields benefits to employers through the productive work of apprentices and because it works as a recruitment tool. For youth apprenticeships, in Israel, many employers may not be able to realise long-term benefits associated with recruitment/retention of the most able apprentices, given that most of the young apprentices enter the IDF. But experience of other countries shows that apprenticeship, if carefully designed, can be beneficial to employers even in the short term, when apprentices are rapidly trained up so that they can be placed in skilled productive work. This implies that Israel should pursue a targeted approach designed to support youth apprenticeship. Two policy options are:

- Expand youth apprenticeships on prestigious occupations, including in public administration, to attract able students to the programme, as discussed in Chapter 2. Support employers in the provision of high-quality apprenticeships by providing services such as mentoring, training for apprentice instructors, help with administrative tasks, and support to employers working with disadvantaged youth.

Israel may also want to expand apprenticeships targeting young people who have completed their military service. Employers are obliged by law to pay the minimum wage to apprentices aged 18 and above which increases the cost of apprenticeship provision in this age group. This may represent a serious barrier to apprenticeship expansion.

- Israel may review its wage setting in line with arrangements encountered in other countries to ensure apprenticeship is beneficial to employers. If this is implemented Israel may analyse the impact of lower wages on individual participation and if necessary, provide additional financial support to apprentices.

Policy arguments: The rationale for reform

Policy argument 1. The economics of youth apprenticeship suggest a twin-pronged approach to their development

Army service is a key determinant of the form of apprenticeship

First, given that most young people are required to serve in the army, youth apprenticeships will normally need to be designed so that apprentices rapidly provide net benefits to employers. This means that their wages need to be modest, while apprentices need to be made productive quickly. An evaluation of costs and benefits of apprenticeships would help to see whether any changes are necessary in the design of the Israeli apprenticeships to reach this objective. Second, for the social groups that are not required to serve in the army, employers providing apprenticeships can count on larger benefits including benefits associated with the productive work of apprentices during the programme but also benefits associated with the recruitment of the best apprenticeship graduates. This is not to suggest that youth apprenticeship should separate the social groups, which would have all kinds of adverse consequences, but it does suggest a realistic approach to the different requirements of the different sub-populations, recognising that the economic attractions of apprenticeship to employers will be variable.

Policy argument 2. The apprentice wage is the most important cost for employers

The wage is a key attraction of youth apprenticeships

In most countries apprentices receive a wage (see Table 3.3). This increases the attractiveness of the programme to young people, as no wage would be received in school-based education (Moretti et al., 2017). Young apprentices who receive a wage are treated like regular employees, they work and are paid for the work done. This can potentially increase their motivation to complete the programme and to carry out with diligence tasks in the work place.

In Israel the youth apprentice wage is relatively low

In Israel, youth apprentices receive around 35% of the skilled worker wage, with some companies paying apprentices more than the minimum required. While this is not very different from other countries, in absolute terms apprentices in Israel earn less than their counterparts in many other countries. This is partly because in Israel apprentices are paid only for their hours with employers while in most other countries the apprentice wage also covers time spent in school. Low apprenticeship wage may also reflect the fact that in Israel apprenticeship is for young people who dropped out from regular school programmes, and such provision is often challenging and thus more costly for employers. This is consistent with evidence from other countries, where the apprentice wage is often lower in programmes catering for disadvantaged youth (Kis, 2016).

Table 3.2. Minimum apprentice wages in youth apprenticeships

	Do apprentices receive wages during the on-the-job period?	Do apprentices receive wage during off-the-job period?	What is the minimum wage the apprentice should receive?	Who defines the minimum apprentice wage?	Do employers pay social security contributions for an apprentice?
Austria	Yes	Yes	On average 50% of the skilled worker wage	Sectors at regional level	Yes, but the state covers parts of the insurance costs
Denmark	Yes	Yes	30-70% of the skilled worker wage, depending on the year of the programme	Sectors	No
Germany	Yes	Yes	25-33% of the skilled worker wage, depending on the year of the programme	Sectors at regional level	Yes
Israel	Yes	No	For youth apprenticeship: 60% of the minimum wage or around 35% of the skilled worker wage1	The minimum apprentice wage is set by law	Missing
Norway	Yes	No : during the first two years provided fully in school Yes : in the last two years with an employer including one year of training	30-80% of the skilled worker wage, depending on the year of the programme	Sectors at national level	Yes
Sweden	No	No	-	-	-
Switzerland	Yes	Yes	On average 20% of the skilled worker wage, depending on the year of the programme	Individual company but employer/ professional associations provide recommendations. As a result apprentice wage varies by sector.	Yes

Note: Apprentice wages can vary largely across sectors and tend to increase over the duration of apprenticeship programme. The apprentice wage in Israel as a share of skilled worker wage was estimated assuming the minimum wage represents 60% of the skilled worker. According to the Income Survey 2011 the average monthly wage of a skilled worker was NIS 6 931, as compared to the minimum wage of NIS 4 100 (Central Bureau of Statistics, 2015).
Source: Kuczera, M. (2017), "Striking the right balance: Costs and benefits of apprenticeship", *OECD Education Working Papers*, No. 153, OECD Publishing, Paris, http://dx.doi.org/10.1787/995fff01-en.

Apprentices of different ages have different wage expectations

The reservation wage (what the potential apprentice would be willing to work for) depends both on environmental factors such as labour market tightness, and individual characteristics such as ability and age. Younger people have lower reservation wages because their immediate needs are low if they still live with their parents, because they expect to recoup their investment in apprenticeship over their lifetime, and because the usual alternative is a school-based programme that offers no wage. By contrast, older apprentices often have families to support, and the alternative to apprenticeship is often a salaried job. In many countries the minimum apprenticeship wage does not depend on age, but for the reasons explained above employers often pay higher wages to older apprentices. In the Netherlands, where two-thirds of apprentices were in employment prior to starting an apprenticeship (most being young adults) three-quarters earn more than the national minimum wage (Christoffels, Cuppen, and Vrielink, 2016). In Switzerland, where the apprentice wage increases over the course of a programme, employers often pay adult apprentices the equivalent of the apprentice wage in the last year of training - about 72% of the median wage of an unqualified worker (Mühlemann, forthcoming).

In Israel apprentice over 18 must receive at least the national minimum wage

In Israel, employers are obliged by law to pay at least the national minimum wage to apprentices over 18. But, unlike many other countries Israeli apprentices 18 and above do not receive the pay while in college. Overall, and even though the wage does not cover the classroom period, the provision of apprenticeship to adults in Israel is expensive to employers in comparison to other countries, and the apprentice salary accounts for a large share of this cost. This might represent a drag on the expansion of apprenticeships.

In many countries apprentice wages are often determined sectorally

Costs and benefits of apprenticeship provision differ largely across sectors (Kuczera, 2017). For this reason in many countries apprenticeship wages are negotiated at the sectoral level. In many other countries, regular worker and apprentice salaries are negotiated by individual sectors (see Table 3.2).

Table 3.3. How the minimum apprentice wage is determined

	Level at which the minimum apprentice wage is determined
Australia	Sectors at national and regional level. In some cases it is up to individual companies
Austria	Sectors at regional level
Denmark	Sectors
England (UK)	National
Germany	Sectors at regional level
Netherlands	Sectors
Norway	Sectors at national level
Scotland	National
Switzerland	Unregulated but in practice sectoral/industry bodies provide recommendations on the wage level that are observed by individual employers

Source: Adapted from Kuczera, M. (2017), "Striking the right balance: Costs and benefits of apprenticeship", *OECD Education Working Papers*, No. 153, http://dx.doi.org/10.1787/995fff01-en.

Policy argument 3. Several additional measures support apprenticeship

Regulations ensure apprentices receive good quality training but increase immediate employer cost

As argued earlier, while the apprentice wage should remain low enough to make apprenticeship attractive to employers, regulation is necessary to avoid the risk that apprentices will be used just as cheap labour. Such regulation should ensure that apprentices have the opportunity to develop a wide range of skills with the employer, and that they receive instruction and carry out skilled productive work, in addition to unskilled work. Israel has in place detailed regulations regarding the work-based learning part, including its content, competences of mentors working with apprentices in companies, and external supervision (Ben Rabi et al., forthcoming). This is a strong point of the Israeli apprenticeship system. But (Ben Rabi et al., forthcoming) point out that some of the existing regulations are not respected by employers because of budgetary constraints. For example, mentors working with apprentices in companies do not receive much training because of the high cost of such a training to employers. Providing training for mentors is particularly challenging for small employers.

Government can support employers by making employers better at training

One way of promoting apprenticeship by governments is to assist employers with providing good quality training and meeting regulatory requirements. This includes measures helping employers with the training of mentors, administrative tasks, and support employers who offer apprenticeships to disadvantaged young people. The objective is to maintain effective regulation in a positive way, by helping employers to comply with regulation, often in their own interest. These measures might be particularly helpful to small companies as they often have limited training experience and cannot comply with all the requirements. (see Box 3.1 on how countries support training of apprentice supervisors in the work place).

> **Box 3.1. Country examples of training for apprentice supervisors in the workplace**
>
> **Germany:** Those who supervise apprentices (typically holders of an upper-secondary qualification) have to pass the trainer aptitude exam, while those with an advanced VET qualification (e.g. master craftsperson) already fulfil the requirements, since master craftsperson programmes include this element (BIBB, 2009a).
>
> In the trainer aptitude exam (*Ausbildereignungsprüfung*), candidates demonstrate their ability to assess educational needs, plan and prepare training, assist in the recruitment of apprentices, deliver training and prepare the apprentice to complete their training (BIBB, 2009a). To prepare for the exam, candidates typically attend "Training for trainer" courses (*Ausbildung für Ausbilder*). These preparatory courses are provided by the chambers of commerce and normally last for 115 hours (BIBB, 2009b). Average costs are EUR 180 for the exam and up to EUR 420 for the preparatory course. Candidates may be supported by their employers and can seek financial support from the state through schemes such as the training credit (*Bildungsprämie*) (TA Bildungszentrum, 2015).

> **Norway:** Optional training is offered to employees involved in supervising apprentices. Some counties provide the training themselves, others ask schools or training offices (which are owned by companies collectively) to ensure its provision. The courses are free to participants since counties provide the course, learning material, subsistence and travel expenses. However, the firm is responsible for the supervisor's pay during the course. Typically, the duration of the training is two days (or four half days) per year. Often there is a time interval between each training session, so that supervisors may practice what they have learnt and prepare a report, which is then presented at the next session. National guidelines, developed in co-operation with VET teacher-training institutions, are available on the Internet and can be adapted to local needs. The form of training typically includes role-play and practice. Supervisors learn to cover the curriculum, complete evaluation procedures and administrative forms, prepare a training plan for apprentices, and follow through the plan.
>
> **Switzerland:** Apprentice supervisors are required to complete a targeted training programme, in addition to having a vocational qualification and at least two years of relevant work experience. Cantons are in charge of training, either by offering courses themselves or by delegating them to accredited training providers. They also subsidise these courses, which are offered in two formats leading to different qualifications (40 hour course costing Swiss Franc [SFR] 600 or 100 hour course costing SFR 2 300). The training courses cover information about the Swiss VET system, vocational pedagogy and how to handle potential problems that may arise with young people (e.g. drugs, alcohol).
>
> *Sources*: ABB (n.d.), "Lehraufsicht", Amt für Berufsbildung und Berufsberatung, Thurgau, Amt für Berufsbildung und Berufsberatung, www.abb.tg.ch/xml_63/internet/de/application/d10079/d9739/f9309.cfm (accessed 26 February 2016); SBFI (n.d.), "Berufsbildungsverantwortliche", Staatssekretariat für Bildung, Forschung und Innovation, www.sbfi.admin.ch/berufsbildung/ (accessed 26 February 2016). BIBB (2009a), Ausbilder-Eignungsverordnung Vom 21 January 2009, Bundesgesetzblatt Jahrgang 2009 Teil I Nr. 5, www.bibb.de/dokumente/pdf/ausbilder_eignungsverordnung.pdf; BIBB (2009b), "Empfehlungen des Hauptausschusses des Bundesinstituts für Berufsbildung zum Rahmenplan für die Ausbildung der Ausbilder und Ausbilderinnen", www.bibb.de/dokumente/pdf/HA135.pdf; TA Bildungszentrum (2015), "Ausbildungs eignungsprüfung IHK (AEVO)", www.ta.de/ausbildereignungspruefung-ihk-aevo.html; Norwegian Directorate for Education and Training (2009), personal communication (22 January 2009).

Policy argument 4. Short 'taster' work-based programmes are less burdensome but also lead to fewer benefits

Chapter 2 recommends mandatory work placements in technological programmes. Some short work placements – often weeks or months - aim to familiarise students with the work environment and an occupation rather than to teach a student a full range of skills required by an occupation. The costs involved in offering work placements are different from those in apprenticeships, with often a smaller administrative burden, no wage costs and fewer demands on the time of the firm's employees. For employers the expected benefits are also different from apprenticeships. Students typically do not perform much productive work during their placements. Yet, employers providing shorter work placements may benefit from getting to know potential recruits, and they may want to interest potential future recruits in a given occupation or a firm. Participating firms may also benefit indirectly, through contact with local vocational schools, and communicating their skills needs to schools.

Policy option 3.2: Sharing cost of training among employers

Low productivity and skills shortages in several economic sectors are holding back Israel's economic growth. While employers would collectively benefit from more workforce training, it is not always in the individual interest of an employer to offer training. To overcome this barrier, and create the step change necessary to improve the supply of skills, Israel may wish to support the establishment of sectoral training levies initiated by social partners, which have been used successfully in some European countries.

Policy arguments: The rationale for reform

Policy argument 1. Financial incentives aim to increase the provision of training

Financial incentives are justified through the collective benefits of training

Financial incentives for companies to train, funded through general public expenditure, are justified when such training leads to positive 'externalities'. Externalities are created when work-based learning yields benefits to employers other than the employer who provided the apprenticeship (e.g. by improving the skills of potential recruits) and to the whole society (by increasing the overall level of human capital). These externalities mean that, in the absence of subsidy, employers would provide insufficient training. This is because although society collectively benefits from this training, the individual employers making the training decision only benefit in a more limited way. Sometimes, these externality benefits fall mainly to employers in the same economic sector, who benefit collectively from a better trained workforce. In this case, an alternative approach is to use training levies.

Financial incentives should be carefully evaluated

Given evidence that programmes with work-based learning represent a cost-effective way of developing workforce skills and transitioning young people smoothly from school to work, many governments support provision of work placements through a range of incentives. See Table 3.2 for a description of some country schemes. Overall, the evidence is that these incentives usually have a modest impact, taking into account deadweight loss (training that would be provided even without the subsidy) and displacement effects (replacing unsubsidised training with other forms of training that qualify for subsidy but are otherwise quite similar). These initiatives should therefore be carefully evaluated to avoid inefficiencies.

Table 3.4. Financial incentives to companies providing apprenticeships

	Tax incentives*	Subsidy	Levy scheme
Australia	Tax incentives depend on the qualifications the programme leads to.	Subsidy in specific cases e.g. person being trained has a disability.	No
Austria	Tax incentives abolished in 2008 and replaced by targeted subsidies.	From 2008 targeted subsidies, have been available per apprentice (the amount depends on the year of apprenticeship), for additional training, for training of instructors, for apprentices excelling on final assessment, for measures supporting apprentices with learning difficulties, and equal access for women to apprenticeships.	A levy fund in the construction sector covering all regions and a levy fund in the electro-metallic industry of one province (Vorarlberg), both negotiated by employers and trade unions.
Belgium – Flanders	Payroll tax deduction.	Direct subsidy depending on the number of apprentices and programme duration.	No
Germany	No	No	In the construction sector. Negotiated by employers and trade unions.
Netherlands	Tax exemptions (abolished in 2014).	From 2014, subsidy to employers up to EUR 2 700 per apprentice per year (depending on the duration of the apprenticeship).	No
Norway	No	Direct subsidy depending on the number of training places, equity role (e.g. to encourage enterprises to take up disadvantaged trainees), and sector.	No
Switzerland	No	No	All companies within certain economic sectors can decide to contribute to a corresponding vocational fund (to develop training, organise courses and qualifications procedures, promote specific occupations).

Note: Tax incentives reduce either the tax base or the tax due. They include: (a) tax allowances (deducted from the gross income to arrive at the taxable income); (b) tax exemptions (some income is exempted from the tax base); (c) tax credits (sums deducted from the tax due); (d) tax relief (some classes of taxpayers or activities benefit from lower rates); (e) tax deferrals (postponement of tax payments).
Source: Adapted from Kuczera, M. (2017), "Striking the right balance: Costs and benefits of apprenticeship", *OECD Education Working Papers*, No. 153, http://dx.doi.org/10.1787/995fff01-en.

Policy argument 2. Sometimes employers share the cost of training

Employers have particular incentives to share the cost of training through levy schemes when the cost of apprenticeship training is high, the labour market is tight and it is difficult to find skilled employees on the external market, and when employers face a high risk that their fully trained employees will be poached by other employers. All these factors can now be identified in Israel.

Across countries training levies have diverse characteristics

Training levies involve a levy on a percentage of employer turnover or payroll, according to certain rules, which is then used to fund training. For example, in Denmark and France, all employers share the cost of apprenticeships through a training levy. In Austria,

Germany and Switzerland, levies are collected by sectors. In the new national system in the United Kingdom, only larger employers contribute. The cost sharing among employers may be initiated by the government [e.g. France, England (United Kingdom)] or by employers themselves (e.g. Austria, Germany and Switzerland). See Box 3.2 for a description of the Swiss scheme. Employers tend to be more sceptical of levy schemes initiated by the government, often perceived by employers as a tax, and where companies have little control over how the money is used and spent (Müller and Behringer, 2012).

Box 3.2. Sectoral training levies in Switzerland

Professional organisations can request the Federal Council to set up a mandatory sectoral fund with all companies in the sector paying solidarity contributions for provision of vocational education and training (e.g. development of regulations, promotion of VET among young people, organisation of professional assessments, development of pedagogical and teaching materials). The contribution depends on the company payroll. In 2008 there were 13 such funds with 16% of Swiss companies participating (SEFRI, 2009). Currently, nearly 30 funds are in place (SEFRI, 2017). Companies contributing to these funds reported that role of the fund was to increase solidarity in sharing the cost of vocational education in the specific sector/industry. Participating companies more or less agreed that the funds fulfilled well their statutory obligations. An evaluation of the funds showed that setting up of these mandatory funds is easier in sectors/industries that are well organised, that the administrative cost of contributing to the fund incurred by the company should be as low as possible and that the use of funds should be transparent (SEFRI, 2009). A robust evaluation of the impact of the funds on apprenticeship provision and its outcomes has not been performed yet.

Source: SEFRI (2009), "Évaluation des fonds en faveur de la formation professionnelle." www.sbfi.admin.ch/sbfi/fr/home/bildung/berufsbildungssteuerung-und--politik/berufsbildungsfinanzierung/fonds-en-faveur-de-la-formation-professionnelle-selon-art--60-lf/evaluation-des-fonds-en-faveur-de-la-formation-professionnelle.html.
SEFRI (2017), "Fonds en faveur de la formation professionnelle entrés en vigueur selon l'art. 60 LFPr", www.sbfi.admin.ch/sbfi/fr/home/bildung/berufsbildungssteuerung-und--politik/berufsbildungsfinanzierung/fonds-en-faveur-de-la-formation-professionnelle-selon-art--60-lf/fonds-en-faveur-de-la-formation-professionnelle-entres-en-vigueu.html.

Employer commitment to sectoral levies can be high

Sectoral levies are driven by employers in industrial sectors where employers see collective advantages from pooling training efforts. They can foster a close relationship between training and employer-defined skills needs in the sector. However, such levies tend to be concentrated in sectors where employers are well organised and have a strong commitment to training (such as construction and engineering), so the capacity of sectoral arrangements to address skills weaknesses in other areas – for example retail and other service industries, is weaker. Sectoral funding may also neglect common core skills which are transferable across industries, and may be ill-adapted to regional needs (Ziderman, 2003; CEDEFOP, 2008).

How the cost of levy is distributed

Levies imply an extra cost for companies that may be absorbed by employers, passed on to customers through higher prices, or shifted on to workers and apprentices through lower wages. If there are many skilled workers willing to work for the company, even at a lower wage, the employer can shift the cost to the workers. If, however, companies struggle to find qualified labour, they may not be able to lower salaries.

Policy argument 3. In Israel employers may need to invest more in training to address skills shortages

There may be insufficient training on-the-job

There is some evidence that in Israel there is insufficient on-the-job training. Just over one-third of 16-65 year-olds report that they have received some on-the-job training, compared with around half their counterparts in many OECD countries (see Figure 3.2). In the smaller firms, relatively few workers report that they receive on-the-job training (see Figure 3.3). One limitation of these data is that they do not record training intensity, i.e. how much on-the-job training is received by those who do receive it.

Figure 3.2. On-the-job training

Percentage of 16-65 year-olds reporting that they received some on-the-job training in the past year

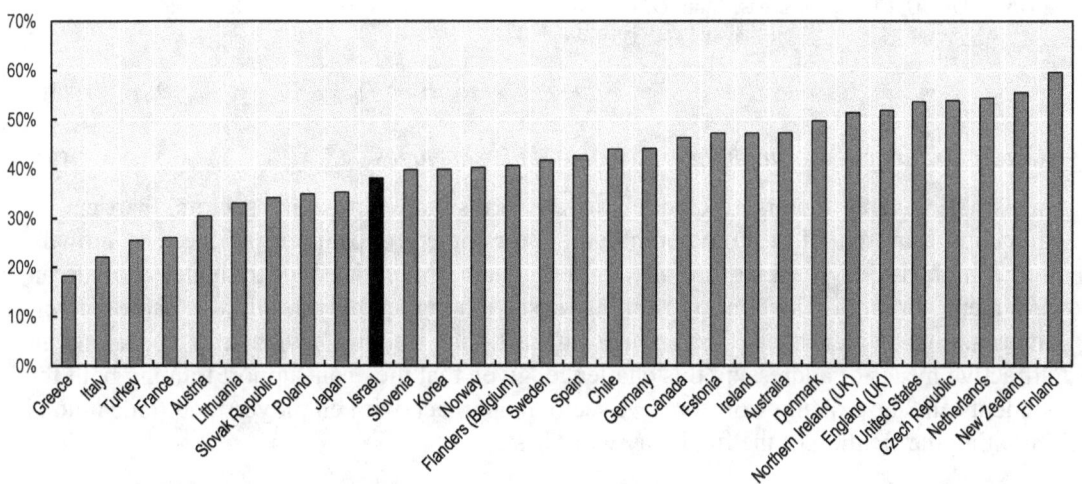

Source: OECD calculations based on *OECD Survey of Adult Skills (PIAAC)* (Database 2012, 2015), www.oecd.org/site/piaac/publicdataandanalysis.htm.

StatLink http://dx.doi.org/10.1787/888933734892

Figure 3.3. Provision of training in Israel, by company size

Share of employees (16-65 year-olds) in Israel reporting participating in on-the-job training in the past year, by company size

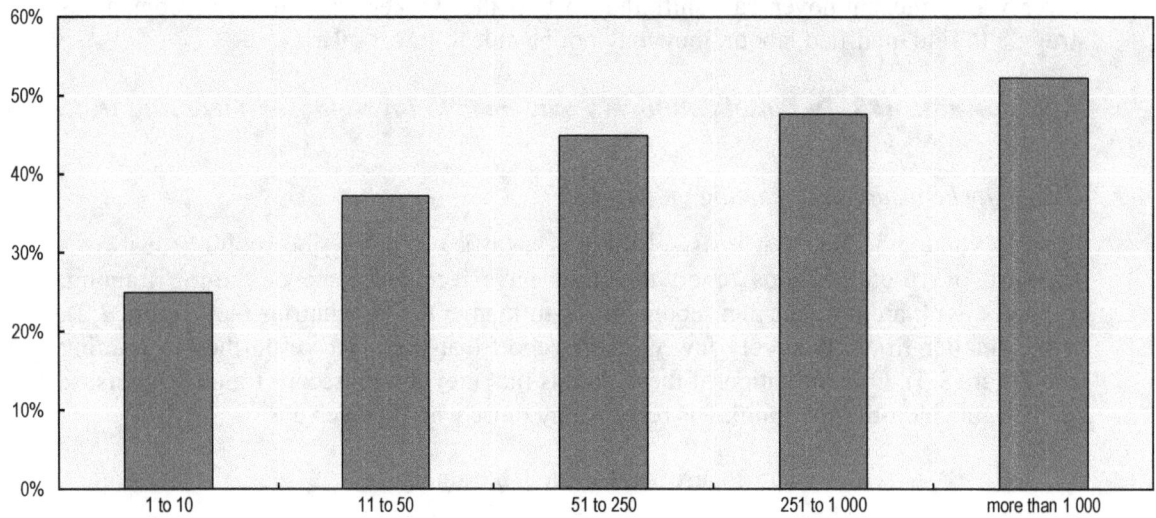

Source: OECD calculations based on *OECD Survey of Adult Skills (PIAAC)* (Database 2012, 2015), www.oecd.org/site/piaac/publicdataandanalysis.htm.

StatLink http://dx.doi.org/10.1787/888933734911

Sectoral training levies might help to tackle skills shortages

In Israel, several factors, including severe skills gaps in some sectors, barriers to transition from school to skilled employment for some groups, poor productivity growth, and a high risk of poaching of fully trained young apprenticeship graduates provide an argument for a distribution of training costs among employers in the same sector. International evidence and experience suggest that training levies may represent an attractive means of addressing this challenge, given that they can support training both for students and the existing workforce. A sectoral approach with employers and trade unions initiating the creation of the fund may work best.

Sectoral training levies might be piloted in economic sectors with serious skills shortages

In Israel, it would make sense to pilot training levies in sectors where the majority of employers favour measures to improve skills supply. The principle is to back the voluntary commitment of a majority of employers to legislation that then mandates the levy on all the employers in the sector (possibly with exemptions for smaller employers). Having established the training fund through this measure, rules for expenditure of this fund can then be established. It might be used to support the training of the existing workforce, including apprentices. For example, in Denmark, the proceeds of the training levy are used to provide wages to apprentices during their time spent on off-the-job training. There is extensive European experience in these types of sectoral levy (CEDEFOP, 2008).

References

ABB (n.d.), "Lehraufsicht", Amt für Berufsbildung und Berufsberatung, Thurgau, Amt für Berufsbildung und Berufsberatung, www.abb.tg.ch/xml_63/internet/de/application/d10079/d9739/f9309.cfm (accessed 26 February 2016).

Ben Rabi, D. et al. (forthcoming), *Apprenticeship and Work-Based Learning in Israel. Background Report for Israel Project: Aiming High – Review of Apprenticeship*.

BIBB (2009a), Ausbilder-Eignungsverordnung Vom 21 January 2009, Bundesgesetzblatt Jahrgang 2009 Teil I Nr. 5, www.bibb.de/dokumente/pdf/ausbilder_eignungsverordnung.pdf.

BIBB (2009b), "Empfehlungen des Hauptausschusses des Bundesinstituts für Berufsbildung zum Rahmenplan für die Ausbildung der Ausbilder und Ausbilderinnen", www.bibb.de/dokumente/pdf/HA135.pdf.

Christoffels, I., J. Cuppen and S. Vrielink (2016), *Verzameling notities over de daling van de bbl en praktijkleren - Rapport - Rijksoverheid.nl, Rapport*, ECBO, MOOZ, www.rijksoverheid.nl/documenten/rapporten/2016/10/18/verzameling-notities-over-de-daling-van-de-bbl-en-praktijkleren.

CEDEFOP (2008), "Sectoral training funds in Europe", *European Center for the Development of Vocational Training Panorama Series*, No.156, Luxembourg.

Central Bureau of Statistics (2015), "Tables from Publication 'Income Survey 2011. Gross Income per Employee, by Occupation (1994 Classification) and Sex, Table 20" www.cbs.gov.il/reader/cw_usr_view_SHTML?ID=570.

Franz, W. and D. Soskice (1994), "The German apprenticeship system", *Discussion Paper,* No. 11 Center for International Labor Economics, University of Konstanz, www.econstor.eu/bitstream/10419/92436/1/720918545.pdf.

Kis, V. (2016), "Work-based learning for youth at risk: Getting employers on board", *OECD Education Working Papers*, No. 150, OECD Publishing, Paris, http://dx.doi.org/10.1787/5e122a91-en.

Kuczera, M. (2017), "Incentives for apprenticeship", *OECD Education Working Papers*, No. 152, OECD Publishing, Paris, http://dx.doi.org/10.1787/55bb556d-en.

Moretti, L., et al. (2017), "So similar and yet so different: A comparative analysis of a firm's cost and benefits of apprenticeship training in Austria and Switzerland", *IZA Discussion Paper*, No. 11081, Institute for the Study of Labor (IZA), https://econpapers.repec.org/paper/izaizadps/dp11081.htm.

Mühlemann S. (forthcoming), "Apprenticeships training for adults: theoretical considerations and empirical evidence for selected OECD members".

Mühlemann, S. (2016), "The Cost and Benefits of Work-based Learning", *OECD Education Working Papers*, No. 143, OECD Publishing, Paris, http://dx.doi.org/10.1787/5jlpl4s6g0zv-en.

Müller, N. and F. Behringer (2012), "Subsidies and levies as policy instruments to encourage employer-provided training", *OECD Education Working Papers*, No. 80, OECD Publishing, Paris, http://dx.doi.org/10.1787/5k97b083v1vb-en.

OECD (2018), *OECD Survey of Adult Skills (PIAAC)* (Database 2012, 2015), www.oecd.org/site/piaac/publicdataandanalysis.htm.

Ryan, P., et al. (2013), "Apprentice pay in Britain, Germany and Switzerland: Institutions, market forces and market power", *European Journal of Industrial Relations,* Vol.19/3, pp. 201-20, https://doi.org/10.1177/0959680113494155.

SBFI (n.d.), "Berufsbildungsverantwortliche", Staatssekretariat für Bildung, Forschung und Innovation, www.sbfi.admin.ch/berufsbildung/ (accessed 26 February 2016).

SEFRI (2015), « Plan de formation relatif à l'ordonnance du SEFRI sur la formation professionnelle initiale de, Electronicienne CFC / Electronicien CFC » , Version 2.0 du 9 novembre 2015, numéro de la profession 46505, www.swissmechanic.ch/documents/ET_Plan_de_formation_V20_151216.pdf.

SEFRI (2009), "Évaluation des fonds en faveur de la formation professionnelle", www.sbfi.admin.ch/sbfi/fr/home/bildung/berufsbildungssteuerung-und--politik/berufsbildungsfinanzierung/fonds-en-faveur-de-la-formation-professionnelle-selon-art--60-lf/evaluation-des-fonds-en-faveur-de-la-formation-professionnelle.html (accessed 25 July 2017).

SEFRI (2017), "Fonds en faveur de la formation professionnelle entrés en vigueur selon l'art. 60 LFPr", www.sbfi.admin.ch/sbfi/fr/home/bildung/berufsbildungssteuerung-und--politik/berufsbildungsfinanzierung/fonds-en-faveur-de-la-formation-professionnelle-selon-art--60-lf/fonds-en-faveur-de-la-formation-professionnelle-entres-en-vigueu.html.

TA Bildungszentrum (2015), "Ausbildungseignungsprüfung IHK (AEVO)", www.ta.de/ausbildereignungspruefung-ihk-aevo.html.

Wolter, S. and P. Ryan (2011), *Apprenticeship Handbook of Economics of Education*, Ed. by R. Hanushek, S. Machin, L. Woessmann, Vol. 3, Elsevier, North-Holland.

Ziderman, A. (2003), "Financing vocational training to meet policy objectives: Sub-Saharan Africa", *African Region Human Development Working Paper Series*, The World Bank, Washington, DC.

Chapter 4. Creating a coherent and transparent vocational education and training system in Israel

> *The vocational system needs to be coherent, with clear relationships between different vocational education and training (VET) programmes, and clear routes of transfer and progression between vocational training and general education programmes. This allows individuals to make the right choice of educational path and helps employers to understand and relate to the different vocational programmes. This chapter argues that to make the system more coherent Israel should give consideration to the creation of a single strategic body that will plan and guide policy development on VET, and champion VET within government. A national qualification framework would also make the system more coherent and transparent. Israel may consider expanding and diversifying provision at post-secondary level, and promote pathways so that vocational choices are not dead ends.*

The statistical data for Israel are supplied by and under the responsibility of the relevant Israeli authorities. The use of such data by the OECD is without prejudice to the status of the Golan Heights, East Jerusalem and Israeli settlements in the West Bank under the terms of international law.

Introduction: Why coherence and transparency matter

This chapter sets out practical steps for the implementation of reform

This chapter argues that action is needed at two different levels. First, the fragmented governance of the system needs be overhauled and simplified, by creating a single strategic body to plan and guide policy development on vocational education and training, to champion VET within government, and to realise a system capable of pursuing policy goals in a systematic and co-ordinated way. A national qualification framework would also make the system more coherent and transparent. Second, efforts are needed to expand and develop the post-secondary vocational system as an alternative to longer studies in academic universities, and to offer higher-level vocational programmes to which graduates of initial VET can naturally aspire.

A strong VET system needs to be coherent and transparent

A successful VET system needs strong individual vocational programmes. But such programmes, in isolation, are not enough. The vocational system also needs to be internally coherent, with clear relationships between different VET programmes, and clear routes of transfer and progression between vocational training and general education programmes. In addition, the vocational system needs to fit with wider social and economic requirements. This coherence and internal logic also need to be transparent to all the stakeholders in the system. That will allow individuals to make choices of relevant vocational programmes, with an eye not only on immediate outcomes, but also on progress from one programme to another and into the labour market. It will also help employers to understand and relate to the different vocational programmes.

Reform to improve coherence and transparency has proved difficult to implement

In Israel, there are large challenges to coherence, given the involvement of multiple government agencies in governance, variable levels of employer engagement, and little sense of a vocational pathway, in which vocational training becomes the entry point for further professional training and individual's career. These issues have been well recognised in Israel, as well as in the OECD's own review (Musset, Kuczera and Field, 2014). A recent report from the National Economic Council (2017) has also recommended several steps, including the systematic development of a qualifications framework, to enhance coherence. Steps are also being taken to relate the occupational certifications developed by the Ministry of Labour, Welfare and Social Services (MLWSS) to the school qualifications delivered in secondary schools under the Ministry of Education. But progress has been slow: while the need for more coherence is clear, making it happen is hard.

Policy option 4.1: Realising coherence in governance

To develop and bring to scale a high-quality VET system, Israel will need to gather information on skills needs, evaluate what is working well and what is not working well within the current system, engage with all the stakeholders, develop a longer-term plan for the development of the vocational system, and secure the required funding. Fragmented governance makes these tasks very difficult.

To drive reform and improve coherence and transparency, Israel may establish an overarching steering body for Israel's vocational education and training system. This body might be called the National Council for Vocational Education and Training.

The National Council should be established on a statutory basis, with its composition and responsibilities set out in law, so as to ensure its authority; it should have its own budget and secretariat; the Council should include representatives of employers, trade unions, government (including from the Ministry of Education and the MLWSS), vocational training institutions, minority groups and wider society.

The main responsibility of the National Council would be to guide the development of the vocational education and training system. To this end, it should:

- Publish a strategic (5-10 year) plan for the development and expansion of vocational education and training in Israel. This plan would be based on an assessment of emerging skills demands, and analysis of how those skills needs are to be met, and the steps which need to be taken by different ministries to meet those demands.

- Ensure that the different programmes and initiatives within the VET sector are evaluated, and publish an annual report, reporting on the contribution of the different elements of the VET system to the longer-term objectives, and making policy recommendations.

- Take direct charge of quality assurance and inspection of vocational provision, replacing the (duplicated and uncoordinated) separate arrangements currently in place. The National Council should also take responsibility for evaluating the quality of the system, and undertake research to this end, reporting this in its annual report.

- Take forward the recommendations of the report of the National Economic Council, guiding the development of a set of information tools to make the vocational system transparent to its users. Such tools would include relevant aspects of a national qualifications framework and strengthened outcome data.

Policy arguments: The rationale for reform

The vocational training system has to respond to the needs and interests of multiple stakeholders, employers in particular, as well as other labour market actors such as trade unions, so that training yields the right skills for employers, and supports individuals over a lifetime career. The engagement of employers ensures that the skillsets embodied in vocational qualifications reflect occupational needs, and that the mix of training provision between different occupations reflects the mix of demand for jobs of different types. At local level, good relationships between the vocational training system and employers help to facilitate work placements for vocational students. Looked at across countries, VET systems therefore maintain a diverse range of bodies to maintain these links at national, regional and sectoral levels. At national level, overarching VET bodies engage the social partners, and typically serve the function of drawing together different government ministries with VET responsibilities.

Policy argument 1: Fragmentation and overlapping responsibilities create inefficiencies

VET falls under the responsibility of different ministries

Although responsibility for most adult vocational education and training rests with the MLWSS, responsibilities at upper-secondary and post-secondary level are shared between MLWSS and the Ministry of Education. Plans to consolidate all upper-secondary vocational schools under the Ministry of Education were dropped in 2016 (ETF, 2017). By law, students must be in classroom education up to the age of 18, unless (according to a special exemption) they enter schools supervised by the MLWSS. In addition, the ministries of health, tourism, and defence all have significant responsibilities in respect of training in their respective sectors (see Table 1.1). Division of responsibilities is a challenge if, as in Israel, different provisions duplicate each other and are poorly connected. One effect of such fragmentation is that many vocational programmes tend to be dead ends, receiving little recognition in the formal education system – for example when qualified practical engineers seek credit recognition on entry to higher education. Students moving across programmes run by various ministries may find it difficult to have their qualifications recognised and to build on knowledge and experience acquired previously.

The demand for stronger co-ordination is long standing

In Israel, the demand for better co-ordination of VET, and some overarching body to deliver that co-ordination, is long standing. Yair, Goldstein and Rotem, (2013) argued that the relationship between the two main ministries should be less competitive and more collaborative, while the State Comptroller of Israel (2010) describes the lack of co-operation between the two ministries as "severely dysfunctional". The Harari commission (Karmi, 2004; Nathanson, Levy and Simanovsky (2010), and the Manufacturer's Association (Lotan, 2010), have all argued for an overarching body to guide vocational education. The report of the German-Israeli Programme on Cooperation in Vocational Education and Training (Pur and Littig, 2017) also argued for a National Authority for VET, with sectoral and other subcommittees, which would operate under the direction of a National Council for VET. The OECD's previous review recommended that Israel "establish a national body involving all the key stakeholders, include the ministries, employers and unions, to provide strategic guidance on the development of the VET system" (Musset, Kuczera and Field, 2014).

But it has often foundered on the challenges of implementation

For a mix of reasons, despite consensus on its necessity, a strong co-ordination body has not yet been established. Many different countries have co-ordination or consultative bodies of one sort or another for VET, but their value and efficacy is highly variable. Co-ordination bodies need something to co-ordinate, and consultative bodies need something to consult on, otherwise these bodies become empty talk shops. This suggests the need not only to establish a mechanism for strategic co-ordination, but also the need for a concrete work plan so its function will be clear, smoothing the path to implementation. The recommendations advanced here are designed to meet this objective. The German-Israeli Programme on Cooperation in Vocational Education and Training report, also set out some quite specific suggestions for the working of a co-ordination body and how it might be structured (Pur and Littig, 2017).

Transferring responsibility for VET to a single Ministry would not solve the co-ordination problems

Since the main responsibility for VET is shared within government by the MLWSS and the Ministry of Education, co-ordination challenges inevitably arise. One option would be to grant one or other Ministry full authority over vocational education and training at both upper-secondary and post-secondary levels. This would have some obvious attractions, as it would solve some problems of co-ordination, and remove some duplication. But whatever the governance of the vocational education and training system, it needs to be effectively integrated into the education system, so that vocational options are taken seriously in primary and lower secondary schools, and so that vocational programmes allow transition into higher education. This means the close engagement of the Ministry of Education and the Council for Higher Education in Israel. Similarly, the vocational education and training system needs to be closely linked to the requirements of industry and employers, and the occupational examinations currently managed by the MLWSS. The implication is that, regardless of the precise allocation of Ministerial responsibilities, the VET system needs strong links both to the Ministry of Education and the MLWSS.

Policy argument 2. A National Council for VET would improve co-ordination in VET

A high-level overarching body in the area of VET is currently missing

In the light of these points, and consistently with many previous studies, this review proposes the establishment of a statutory body, to steer the development of vocational education and training in Israel. This body would be composed of representatives of employers and trade unions as well as government. The Council may also include representatives of the minority groups. Given the scale of entrenched co-ordination challenges in Israel, legislation is essential to establish the role of the National Council, so that its status as the coordinating body for VET becomes unchallengeable, and it has the authority to bring relevant stakeholders together to co-operate. The statutory responsibility of the body to report to the Knesset (Israeli Parliament) and make recommendations for any further legislative change would provide a powerful incentive for all the key stakeholders to co-operate informally within the framework provided by the body. Introduction of the proposed changes would require changes in the law. Drawing on previous Israeli experience this process can be challenging.

A longer-term strategic plan for the development of VET in Israel is important

There are a number of economic demands for skills. These include the need to replace the many technically trained immigrants from the former Soviet Union who are now reaching retirement age, specific needs to provide appropriate training and education for those groups with low rates of economic activity, including the Haredi male and Arab female populations. Other new demands are emerging from the changing shape of Israel's economy. All of these demands need to be quantified, and set against the current and expected future capacity of the vocational training system. This process will help to establish an assessment of the technical and vocational skills which will be required in coming years, and underpin strategic proposals by the National Council for how the vocational system should be developed to meet those needs.

Quality assurance is awkwardly duplicated by the two main ministries

High-level quality assurance is provided by the two main ministries, of education and MLWSS in respect of 'their' schools, currently through two separate inspectorates reporting in parallel. To facilitate convergence in the relevant programmes, and to improve efficiency, it is proposed that the high-level quality assurance should be brought together in a single Inspectorate of vocational education and training programmes under the proposed National Council. A significant part of quality assurance is offered by the school networks themselves and municipal authorities. But quality assurance at the practical level of inspection of teaching and institutions needs to be backed by analysis and evaluation of programmes and policies, and placed in a broader context of wider objectives for the vocational training system. Similarly, analytical research on programmes and policies can be informed by the practical experience of inspectors in schools and colleges. For these reasons it makes good sense to bring both functions under the authority of the National Council. This will also help to ensure convergence and co-ordination of the programmes under the two ministries, as well as creating efficiencies through economies of scale.

Policy argument 3. The national qualifications framework would increases clarity and remove duplications

Establishment of the qualification framework is in line with recommendations of the National Economic Council of Israel

The development of a national qualifications framework was recommended in a previous OECD report (Musset, Kuczera and Field 2014), more recently reinforced by, for example a recent report by the European Training Fund (2017), and by the German-Israeli Programme on Cooperation in Vocational Education and Training (Pur and Littig, 2017) recommendation for a unified certificate system, linked to the European Qualifications Framework. These recommendations are now being taken forward through the work of an Inter-Ministerial committee under the National Economic Council. The National Economic Council report argues that a national qualifications framework now needs to be established, which maps and ranks all national diplomas given in the education and training system of Israel. The aspiration is ambitious, going beyond mere linear ranking of qualifications. The aim is a system which reflects the value of the qualifications, their weight as part of continuing studies and training, and their potential for mobility within and between the professional technological and academic tracks. More specifically, this will involve measures to seek convergence between the Ministry of Education technological tracks and vocational certificates awarded by the MLWSS so that graduates from the technological tracks can also receive vocational certificates. This objective can only be reached if there is a co-operation between the two ministries. Increasing the value of qualifications will also require recognition of training in the IDF to support the further education and training of discharged soldiers and course exemptions for practical engineers wishing to progress into higher education (National Economic Council, 2016). These are commendable objectives.

Many countries have established qualifications frameworks to make the system more transparent

The challenges faced in Israel are not uncommon. VET systems and associated qualifications are often partly managed by a Ministry with education responsibilities, and partly by a Ministry with labour market responsibilities. One effect is that, as in Israel, there are sometimes competing systems of qualification. To address this challenge and to make the system more transparent many countries around the world have introduced, or are introducing national qualifications frameworks. When they encompass both vocational and general education (including higher education), such frameworks can allow vocational and general tracks to grant qualifications that are at the same 'level' within the framework (CEDEFOP, 2016). But many barriers remain, often because National Qualification Frameworks (NQFs) can sometimes formalise barriers between vocational and academic programmes. While frameworks can be helpful in promoting system transparency, they should not be expected to achieve miracles on their own. In practice, in Israel as in other countries, much will depend not just on the qualifications framework, but also on how the qualifications are related to one another and whether they are meaningful to employers and individuals. The National Economic Council is therefore right to set its sights on methods of mutual recognition of qualifications, which will allow, on a case by case basis, for this to take place.

Policy argument 4. Better data would support a coherent and transparent system

Disparate sources of data on VET and its outcomes are not brought together

While various data are available in Israel on the labour market outcomes of VET programmes, these data are not adequately collated and utilised either for the purposes of policy making, operational planning, or for guiding the careers of individuals. ETF (2017) point out that the data sources and surveys are fragmented around different agencies, including the responsible ministries, the Central Bureau of Statistics and the Manufacturing Association. They include labour force surveys, surveys of employer needs, but there is no "system capable of making useful labour market information available to education and training planners" (ETF, 2017). Similarly Pur and Littig (2017) argue that data collection and analysis needs to be much better co-ordinated. One role of the National Council, recommended above, would therefore be to co-ordinate data collection on VET. Israel benefits from having a strong research capacity and many good analysts, able to draw conclusions from these data; but to this end the data need initially to be brought together.

Reliable and timely data support evaluation culture

Better data, collated and analysed systematically, should also help to establish an evaluation culture that should underpin the development of VET. While this report recommends the expansion of VET in Israel on strategic grounds, it should not be done without care, but in a way which respects evidence on whether specific programmes can provide the skills needed by Israel's economy, and improve the life chances of those who graduate. Currently, evaluation is limited, and more systematic co-ordination is required to answer key policy questions. For example, it is very important to know what the relative strengths and weaknesses are of the full apprenticeship programme at upper-secondary level run by the MLWSS, and the one day a week work placement for students in technological programmes managed by the Ministry of Education.

Policy option 4.2: Developing post-secondary options

As argued in Chapter 2, the current system works well for students following prestigious technological programmes and demand of high-level skills in Israel is growing. As a result, upper-secondary vocational training in the form of apprenticeships may expand somewhat, but is not likely to be an option for a large proportion of the cohort. More academically demanding technological sub-tracks will remain more academic, and will not make school-leavers job-ready in respect of individual jobs or careers. While upper-secondary VET programmes can and should be constructively developed, much of the burden of expanding vocational education and training will therefore fall on post-secondary programmes.

In Israel many young people fail to obtain the Bagrut and many do not enter higher education. The offer for these young people is currently weak. Israel's economic performance, and social cohesion depends on giving these young people relevant working skills and integrating them into the labour market. Israel may consider expanding and diversifying provision at post-secondary level, and promote pathways so that vocational choices are not dead ends. This implies action at three levels:

- The offer of short post-secondary vocational programmes needs to be diversified and expanded, and funded on the same basis as higher education in the interests of both efficiency and fairness.
- A strengthened institutional foundation should be established by promoting much fuller co-operation between the technical and academic colleges, and in some cases mergers. This co-operation should be used to diversify the offer of one and two-year post-secondary vocational programmes beyond the current technical areas.
- To secure the status of post-secondary vocational programmes, and to meet skill needs, these programmes need to sustain the option of subsequent progression to higher education.

Policy arguments: The rationale for reform

Globally, developed countries display a growing demand for post-secondary vocational qualifications, with some advanced countries graduating 20-30% of the cohort at this level (OECD, 2014). There is nothing in Israel on the demand side that could explain the small size of this sector. The strong labour market demand for skills associated with a wave of retirements affecting the migrants who came from the Soviet Union in the early 1990s, and typically entered higher-level technical jobs, create a historic opportunity to promote post-secondary VET. In the previous OECD review, Musset, Field and Kuczera (2014) identified two key factors deterring people from entering vocational programmes – first, vocational tracks at upper-secondary level are often dead ends, with very limited options for progress to higher-level programmes, and second, there are large barriers in transitioning from practical engineering programmes to higher education. It recommended steps to improve the access of upper-secondary VET graduates to further learning opportunities, including post-secondary VET; and enhance access to universities and credit recognition for graduates of practical engineering programmes. Building on these recommendations, the National Economic Council (2016) proposes a 'continuum of advanced studies' for practical engineers. Pur and Littig (2017) propose the creation of a set of higher-level qualifications for graduate apprentices, including the equivalent of a German Meister qualification (equivalent of a post-secondary qualification). This review seeks to build on previous work, and present suggestions for the further development of post-secondary vocational programmes in Israel.

There are multiple barriers to expansion of post-secondary VET

A number of barriers fall between the set of programmes and institutions providing technician and practical engineering programmes on the one hand, and higher education in academic colleges on the other. First, governance: the technical colleges fall mainly under the authority of the MLWSS, while the academic colleges are accredited by the Council for Higher Education in Israel. Consequently, only the academic colleges are 'higher' education, and use the terminology of 'academic' education. Second, funding: academic colleges and universities are funded much more generously. Third, coverage: many fields of study are not at present available in the practical engineering and technician programmes. Fourth, progression: as described in Musset, Field and Kuczera (2014), progression from practical engineering and technician programmes to bachelors' programmes in universities, and obtaining credit for what has already been learnt, is fraught with difficulty. These factors provide a highly effective means of institutionalising an artificial divide, and with it the low status of the practical engineering and technician programmes. These specific points are addressed in more detail below.

Policy argument 1. Post-secondary VET is not part to the higher education system

Israel currently maintains two 'college' systems in parallel

As described in Chapter 1, 70 technical colleges currently provide two-year practical engineering and one-year technician programmes to around 13 000 students while 37 'academic' colleges, and 21 academic teacher-training colleges provide bachelors level and some masters programmes to around 100 000 students. A very few colleges – for example the ORT Braude College of Engineering - provide both types of programme, but this is the exception to the rule – despite the fact that many of the academic colleges deliver technical programmes and both types of college are in the business of providing post-secondary education in technical and professional areas.

Much stronger collaboration between the two college sectors is needed

Standing back from the specifics, there are, as argued above, grounds for believing that Israel needs a revitalised post-secondary sector, with a range of short vocational programmes, and not just in the technical areas which currently dominate provision in practical engineering and technician programmes. Developing such programmes will require much more effective co-operation between the two 'college' sectors. Currently, the academic colleges provide programmes in subjects such as art and design, communication, business administration, law, and tourism areas where there is much scope for shorter vocational programmes, and, as argued above, for certain jobs, there is no need for a full bachelor's programme. Developing programmes in these areas will naturally involve drawing on the expertise of the existing academic colleges, and in some areas, much fuller co-operation between the sectors. It will also facilitate credit recognition, for example when a graduate of a one or two-year programme wishes to continue their studies and complete a bachelor's degree. In some areas, it may make sense to merge the functions, as in community colleges in the United States (see Box 4.1).

> **Box 4.1. Community colleges in the United States**
>
> Community colleges in the United States bring together two functions, associated with two different lines of historical development. One was the early 20th century growth of "junior colleges," designed to provide students with the first two years of a bachelor's degree education, leaving universities to focus on the more rigorous last two years. The second was the establishment of two-year technical institutes designed for post-high-school vocational preparation. Some institutions specialise in one or other function, but most community colleges deliver both.
>
> Community colleges typically serve multiple missions, including preparation for 4-year education, workforce development, and adult basic education. In addition to VET, their offerings typically include non-credit courses and community services, non-credit federally

> supported workforce training, remedial education, fine and cultural arts, and general education and transfer courses. But both within and across states, community colleges vary widely in their focus on these goals. About 80% of community college students are enrolled to earn an associate's degree, with about 10% seeking a certificate, and another 10% not seeking a credential.
>
> Community colleges tend to be adaptable institutions, which makes it easy for them to respond to local education and training needs, but at the cost of having their mission under constant scrutiny and subject to change. Although most analysts credit the community college with playing a vital role in increasing access to post-secondary education, providing valuable workforce training opportunities, and serving local needs for a variety of adult learning activities, these institutions have historically been viewed as "lower tier". In part, some of this image problem may stem from community colleges historical roots as "junior" colleges. But they are also less "prestigious" by design—they have open admissions, educate students who lack basic educational or occupational skills or are otherwise not prepared for 4-year college, focus on teaching rather than research, and award primarily sub-baccalaureate credentials.
>
> There are high rates of drop-out, but even those who drop out often seem to get some returns from their studies, and those who do graduate with a two-year associates degree or a shorter certificate earn 10-20% more than those with no post-secondary education.
>
> *Source*: U.S. Department of Education, Institute of Education Sciences, National Center for Education Statistics, Career/Technical Education Statistics (2013), *U.S. Background Information Prepared for the OECD Post-secondary Vocational Education and Training "Skills Beyond School" Study*, Washington, http://nces.ed.gov/surveys/ctes/pdf/PostsecVET.pdf; Kuczera, M. and S. Field (2013), *A Skills beyond School Review of the United States*, OECD Reviews of Vocational Education and Training, http://dx.doi.org/10.1787/9789264202153-en.

Policy argument 2. Post-secondary vocational programmes are much less generously funded than higher education

Given the objective of expanding the post-secondary offer, the first step is to ensure that vocational post-secondary programmes are in a position to compete fairly with higher education. Currently, total expenditure, per student year, for higher education college engineering students is much higher than expenditure for practical engineering and technician students in MLWSS institutions (see Table 4.1). The government contribution to those costs is more than three times higher in college engineering degrees. The implication is that teaching intensity and quality is likely to be better in college programmes. These are large differences, so students and their parents will nearly always prefer full bachelors' degrees, regardless of other considerations. The Manufacturing Association has argued that the expansion of academic colleges has creamed off most of the available talent (National Economic Council, 2016). The current funding arrangements also mean that when credit recognition for practical engineering programmes is sought for those who wish to progress to a bachelor's degree, academic colleges and universities have grounds for believing that the quality of tuition received in those programmes is not at the level of much better resourced higher education programmes.

Table 4.1. Funding of practical engineering and technician programmes and 'academic' engineers

Per student/year, NIS, 2017

	Government funding	Tuition fees	Total
Practical engineering and technicians in technical colleges (MLWSS)	9 900	6 960	16 860
Practical engineering (MoE)	19 500	6 479	25 997
Higher Education College degree in engineering	34 300	10 066	44 366

Source: MLWSS (2018), personal communication (23 January 2018).

This imbalance in funding needs to be resolved on grounds both of efficiency and equity

Efficiency requires students to choose the right programme option for their needs, and skills needs in the economy will require some post-secondary graduates with one year of post-secondary studies, some with two years and some with more. But the current framework wastefully shoehorns all but those lacking required prior qualifications (full matriculation) into bachelor programmes. Given that those without the prior qualifications required for higher education are often more disadvantaged, this also acts to magnify education inequity by offering weakly funded programmes to the most disadvantaged. This distortion creates large economic costs.

Substantial investment in post-secondary vocational training is needed

The distortion should be resolved by investing in the quality of practical engineering and technician programmes, substantially increasing yearly expenditure per student to approach the levels of higher education. This should increase the economic efficiency and equity of the post-secondary system. The direct public expenditure costs of the additional expenditure on practical engineering and technician programmes will be offset by encouraging more young people to choose shorter post-secondary programmes rather than bachelors programmes, thus saving public money. Given that there are around 100 000 students in academic colleges, and around 13 000 students currently in practical engineering and technician programmes, the diversion of just a small proportion of those 100 000 students into shorter programmes would create substantial savings. Moreover, for those diverted, there would also be large savings to individuals both in reduced tuition costs, and reduced opportunity costs, since they would enter the labour market one year earlier. The aim is not to reduce course length simply because of the savings involved, but to create a level playing field in which individuals can make efficient decisions about the right type of course for them, without the current very artificial incentives to choose a bachelor's programme.

Policy argument 3. Vocational post-secondary programmes are only provided in technical fields

More appropriate funding would also provide a strong foundation for extending the one and two-year model to a wider range of fields of study, not just the technical fields currently pursued in practical engineering and technician programmes and to provide higher-level programmes to apprentices. Many countries maintain a wide range of short post-secondary programmes in fields such as business, legal studies, tourism and in paramedical occupations. This point is considered further below.

Policy argument 4. Transition from post-secondary programme to into higher education is difficult

The aspiration to enter higher education is widespread

In Israel, as in many OECD countries, increasing numbers of young people aspire to higher education. This reflects increased ambitions among young people, labour market demand for higher-level skills and a need to upskill and reskill throughout life. In response, many young people seek the most direct route to higher education via academic upper-secondary education. Some technological programmes also prepare effectively students for higher education studies, as discussed in Chapter 2. But others, for multiple reasons, may pursue low-level technological programmes and apprenticeships, without necessarily abandoning this aspiration. The implication is that it will be extremely important to establish a clear pathway from VET to post-secondary vocational education and from post-secondary vocational programmes to higher education as a means of meeting student aspirations, and removing any perception of VET tracks as dead ends. Such pathways will help to meet growing economic demands for higher-level skills, support lifelong learning, and promote social inclusion and mobility, by opening up opportunities for higher education to a wider group of people, including the most disadvantaged.

Higher education entrants may come from upper-secondary or post-secondary vocational programmes

The importance of pathways to higher education is widely recognised in Israel, and the 2016 National Economic Council report gives much emphasis to their development. There are two main pathways to higher education at issue: from upper-secondary education; and from post-secondary vocational programmes (such as technician and practical engineering). In Israel, the key issue is transition from youth apprenticeship programmes to higher education and transition and recognition when graduates of practical engineering and technician programmes seek entry to higher education. The first point was addressed in Chapter 2, and this chapter focuses on the last challenge – transition from post-secondary VET to higher education. The challenge in Israel is echoed in many countries, where post-secondary vocational programmes seek recognition for their graduates when entering higher education. Individual vocational institutions can establish bilateral agreements with other education institutions, with rights of access and credit recognition for their graduates. While these bilateral arrangements are relatively common, they consume much administrative energy. Sometimes a national or regional system can facilitate pathways, given the commitment of the participant institutions. In England (United Kingdom), the Skills for Sustainable Communities Lifelong Learning Network established more than 300 progression agreements, mostly between vocational further education colleges and higher education institutions (McKee, n.d.). In Japan, a credit transfer programme encourages universities and junior colleges to exchange credits with professional training colleges (Sawano, 2015). The previous OECD report focusing on post-secondary VET in Israel discussed this issue in detail and provided policy options to tackle it (Musset, Field and Kuczera, 2014).

References

CEDEFOP (2016). *Qualifications Frameworks in Europe*, www.cedefop.europa.eu/mt/publications-and-resources/publications/9117.

ETF (2017), *Israel Country Strategy Paper 2017-20*, www.etf.europa.eu/wpubdocs.nsf/0/5D8ED58F499BEB96C12580BC0056F2B7/$File/CSP%20Israel%202017-2020_External%20Distribution%20Jan%202017.pdf.

Fazekas, M. and I. Litjens (2014), *A Skills beyond School Review of the Netherlands*, OECD Reviews of Vocational Education and Training, OECD Publishing, Paris, http://dx.doi.org/10.1787/9789264221840-en.

Karmi, S. (2004), *The Crisis of Israel Post-Zionist Education: Perceptions and Trends in Conflicts*, HaKibbutz HaMeuchad.

Kuczera, M. and S. Field (2013), *A Skills beyond School Review of the United States*, OECD Reviews of Vocational Education and Training, OECD Publishing, Paris, http://dx.doi.org/10.1787/9789264202153-en.

Lotan, T. (2010), "The Israeli experience of vocational and technical education, and the contribution of employers' organizations to the inclusion of young people in the labour market", in Blanpain, R., (ed.) *Labour Productivity, Investment in Human Capital and Youth Employment: Comparative Developments and Global Responses*, Bulletin of Comparative Labour Relations, No. 73, Kluwer Law International.

McKee, B. (n.d.), *In Practice: Developing Progression Agreements*, SSCLLN Best Practice Guides, www.heacademy.ac.uk/system/files/ssc_developing_progression_agreements.pdf.

Musset, P., M. Kuczera and S. Field (2014), *A Skills beyond School Review of Israel*, OECD Reviews of Vocational Education and Training, OECD Publishing, Paris, http://dx.doi.org/10.1787/9789264210769-en.

Nathanson R., R. Levy and N. Simanovsky (2010), *Proposal for a Vocational Training Model for Israel*, Friedrich-Ebert-Stiftung and the Macro Center for Political Economics.

National Economic Council (2016), *Interministerial Team Report To improve the system of accreditation and mobility between the education and training systems)*, www.pmo.gov.il/BranchesAndUnits/direcgeneral/Pages/Accreditation.aspx.

OECD (2018), *OECD Survey of Adult Skills (PIAAC)* (Database 2012, 2015), www.oecd.org/site/piaac/publicdataandanalysis.htm.

OECD (2014), *Skills beyond School: The Synthesis Report*, OECD Reviews of Vocational Education and Training, OECD Publishing, Paris, http://dx.doi.org/10.1787/9789264214682-en.

Pur, S. and P. Littig (2017), *Promoting Research and Innovation in Vocational Education and Training (VET) in Israel. Final Report on the German-Israeli VET Project 2014 – 2016*, www.na-bibb.de/presse/news/abschlussbericht-der-projektteamkooperation-promoting-research-and-innovation-in-vocational-education-and-training-vet-in-israel/.

Sawano, Y. (2015), "Higher education and lifelong learning in Japan: Why is it so difficult to promote recurrent education?", in , J. Yang, C. Schneller, and S. Roche, (eds.), *The Role of Higher Education in Promoting Lifelong Learning*, UNESCO Institute for Lifelong Learning, Hamburg.

U.S. Department of Education, Institute of Education Sciences, National Center for Education Statistics, Career/Technical Education Statistics (2013), *U.S. Background Information Prepared for the OECD Post-secondary Vocational Education and Training "Skills Beyond School" Study*, Washington, http://nces.ed.gov/surveys/ctes/pdf/PostsecVET.pdf.

Yair, G., K. Goldstein and N. Rotem (2013), *Country Report: Israel, Mapping of VET Educational Policies and Practices for Social Inclusion and Social Cohesion in the Western Balkans, Turkey and Israel*, European Training Foundation.

Chapter 5. Improving literacy and numeracy in vocational education and training (VET) programmes in Israel

The basic skills of numeracy and literacy are positively associated with a range of important economic and social outcomes both for individuals and countries. In Israel, the basic skills of the adult population are weak in comparison to other OECD countries. This chapter argues that, in the context of vocational education and training (VET) programmes, improving the basic skills of Israeli population would lead to economic and non-economic benefits such as stronger productivity and a more equal society. Israel should ensure adequate levels of literacy and numeracy in all VET students, identifying the weakest performers and targeting teaching resources on them to improve their basic skills. Chapter 5 also argues that Israel may build basic skills education systematically into adult programmes. Basic skills are particularly low among Arab Israelis and Haredi Jews. Addressing basis skills weaknesses in the disadvantaged and underperforming populations should be a priority.

The statistical data for Israel are supplied by and under the responsibility of the relevant Israeli authorities. The use of such data by the OECD is without prejudice to the status of the Golan Heights, East Jerusalem and Israeli settlements in the West Bank under the terms of international law.

Introduction: Comparing basic skills in Israel with other countries

Basic skills are important

Basic skills of numeracy and literacy have a major impact on life chances, being positively associated with a range of important economic and social outcomes both for individuals and countries (OECD, 2016; Hanushek et al., 2015 and Grotlüschen et al., 2016). They are also very important in vocational education and training, as jobs require basic, transferable skills, as well as occupation-specific skills. Basic skills also support further learning, and many VET graduates will want to, or need to continue to learn, formally and informally, throughout their lives. This chapter argues that, in the context of VET programmes, improving the basic skills of Israeli adults would lead to economic and non-economic benefits such as stronger productivity and more equal society.

How the low-skilled are defined in this report

In this chapter "low-skilled" is used as shorthand for those who are at or below Level 2 in literacy or numeracy in the Survey of Adult Skills (PIAAC), recognising that they may have good levels of other skills, including practical occupational skills. The skills measured are those of everyday life, such as skills required to read a petrol gauge and understand how to sensibly take painkillers.

Almost two million adults in Israel have low skills

According to the Survey of Adult Skills, around 1.7 million, or 37% of Israeli adults have low levels of literacy or numeracy, or both, well above the OECD average of 27% (see Figure 5.1).

The risk of being low-skilled is higher for Arabs and in traditional and religious Jewish communities

In the Arab population the share of low-skilled is twice as high as among Jews (60% vs. 30%), but even within the Jewish population of Israel, the risk of being low-skilled is higher than the OECD average, with the share of low-skilled in traditional and religious Jewish communities reaching 50%, compared to 20% among non-religious secular Jews. Arab women are the most vulnerable group with around 65% of them being low-skilled, comparing to 31% of Jewish women.

Other characteristics of the low-skilled in Israel

As in other countries, the low-skilled tend to be less educated, come from less advantaged backgrounds and tend to be older. Thus:

- In Israel around 40% of young adults (16-40 year-olds) with below upper-secondary qualifications as their highest qualification (primary school and junior high school) are low-skilled compared to 14% of those with tertiary (university) qualifications.

- The low-skilled are more likely to come from less well educated families nearly everywhere. But the association between family background (measured by parental education) and skills is particularly strong in Israel.

- As in most countries, older Israelis are more likely to be low-skilled. More than half (53%) of those aged 55-65 years are low-skilled, twice the proportion (27%) of 25-34 year-old Israelis. This partly reflects better education among young people, but also other factors.

- According to data from the Survey of Adult Skills two-thirds of the low-skilled in Israel are in work.

Figure 5.1. Israel has a higher proportion of low-skilled adults than most countries

Percentage of the adult population aged 16-65

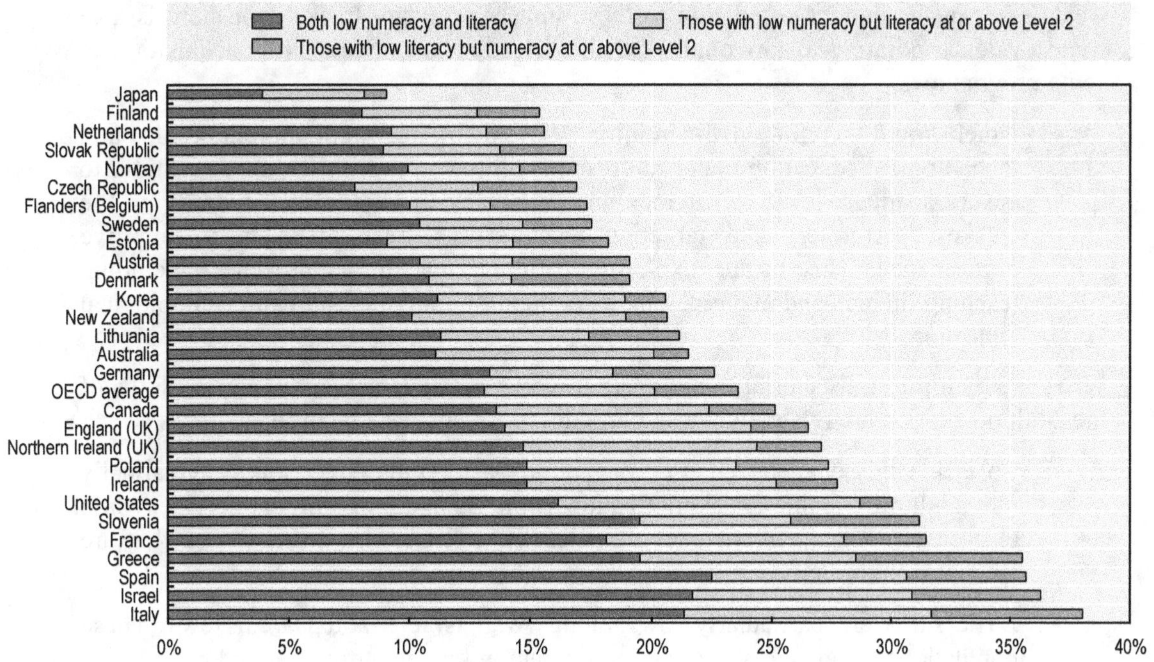

Source: OECD calculations based on OECD *Survey of Adult Skills (PIAAC)* (Database 2012, 2015), www.oecd.org/site/piaac/publicdataandanalysis.htm.

StatLink http://dx.doi.org/10.1787/888933734930

Figure 5.2. Share of low-skilled and absolute numbers in different population groups

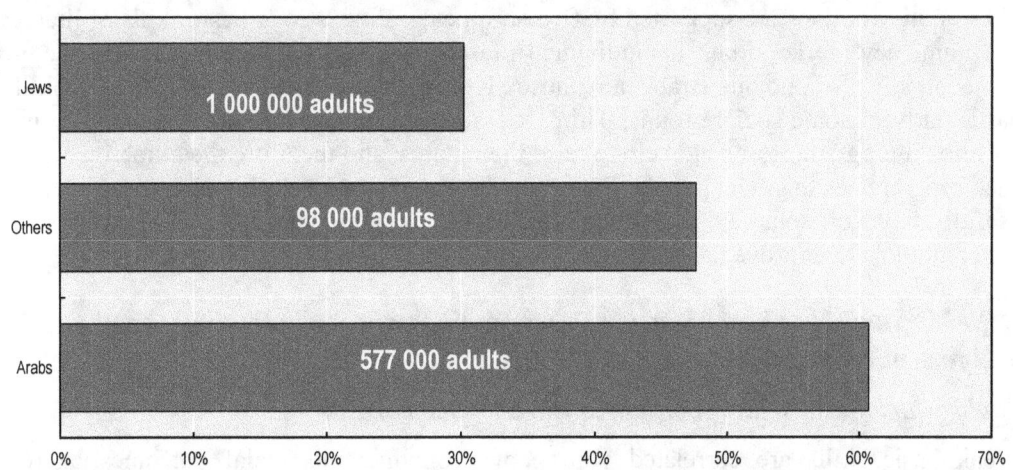

Source: OECD calculations based on OECD *Survey of Adult Skills (PIAAC)* (Database 2012, 2015), www.oecd.org/site/piaac/publicdataandanalysis.htm.

StatLink http://dx.doi.org/10.1787/888933734949

Policy options: Addressing basic skills challenge in VET and apprenticeship programmes

In Israel, a large share of young people leave initial VET with poor basic skills, and this may be one reason why, as explained in Chapter 2, there is no wage premium associated with this qualification. Often, the low basic skills of VET graduates will reflect weaknesses in the entrant population to these upper-secondary tracks. But there is also some evidence pointing to low quality teaching leading to modest skills acquisition in some programmes.

- Israel should therefore invest in initial VET, including youth apprenticeships and technological education under the responsibility of the Ministry of Education, to ensure adequate levels of literacy and numeracy in all students, identifying the weakest performers and targeting teaching resources on them to improve performance. This means exploring different teaching approaches, including teaching literacy and numeracy in the context of apprenticeship and technological education.

There are multiple skills shortages in the adult workforce in Israel, and the basic skills of the adult population are relatively weak, particularly for some social groups.

- To tackle this challenge, Israel may build basic skills education systematically into adult programmes, seeking to address the issue during military service, while also ensuring that effective programmes are in place for those groups that are exempt from military service.
- Basic skills are particularly low among Arab Israelis and Haredi Jews. These populations are also less likely to participate in the labour market and are more at risk of living in poverty. Since basic skills are closely related to the labour market outcomes and life chances addressing basis skills weaknesses in these populations should be a priority.

Policy arguments: The rationale for reform

These policy options are supported by five arguments. First, strong basic skills of literacy and numeracy are important for individual life chances and support the performance of the economy. Second, in Israel, an unusually high share of adults lack basic skills, particularly in some social groups. Third, measures to build basic skills more fully into vocational programmes would help to raise their status, and therefore the attractiveness of such programmes to young people. Fourth, in developing basic skills education, Israel can usefully build on some existing initiatives. Fifth, international evidence suggests some different tools to improve basic skills.

Policy argument 1. Strong basic skills are important for individual life chances and for collective outcomes

Adults with low skills have poor labour market outcomes

Weak basic skills are correlated with poor economic and social outcomes. Across countries, those with weak basic skills are more likely to be unemployed and outside the labour market (OECD, 2016). In Israel 30% of the low-skilled are not in the labour force and not studying compared to 10% among the highly skilled – a finding partly explained by the higher average age of the low-skilled. Two-thirds of the low-skilled in Israel are in work, but they more often work in unskilled and low-paid jobs, and are less satisfied with their job than highly skilled workers. The association between skills and wages is particularly strong in Israel. On average across OECD countries that participated in the survey, the median hourly wage of salaried employees with high numeracy skills (Level 4 or 5) is around 60% higher than that of workers with low numeracy skills. The same is valid for literacy skills. In Israel, this difference is third highest among the participating countries (OECD, 2016: 126). In most countries including Israel people with low levels of skills have poorer health, trust others less and are less likely to engage in community life and democratic processes than high-skilled adults.

Israel needs more skilled workers

Many companies in Israel face shortages of skilled labour, and this is one of the main bottlenecks inhibiting growth and competitiveness (OECD, 2018). While skill needs in Israel were sometimes satisfied through large scale migration in the past, this may be less likely to occur in the future and Israel must therefore seek to upskill the current work force and activate those outside the labour market.

Training measures need to give adequate attention to literacy and numeracy

Training measures should aim to improve the quality and quantity of workforce skills. Given that in Israel around one in three of those in work have low numeracy or literacy skills, (more than most other OECD countries) this task is challenging and needs to be pursued with full attention to basic skills requirements, as well as to specific occupational skills (see Figure 5.3). Stronger basic skills among adults would support the introduction of new technology, and would therefore provide a long-term incentive for firms to increase the stock of physical capital (buildings, machinery and equipment) per worker and to increase efficiency through technological innovation (Bank of Israel, n.d.).

Figure 5.3. The Israeli workforce includes a large share of low-skilled

Share of low-skilled among those in employment (16-65 year-olds)

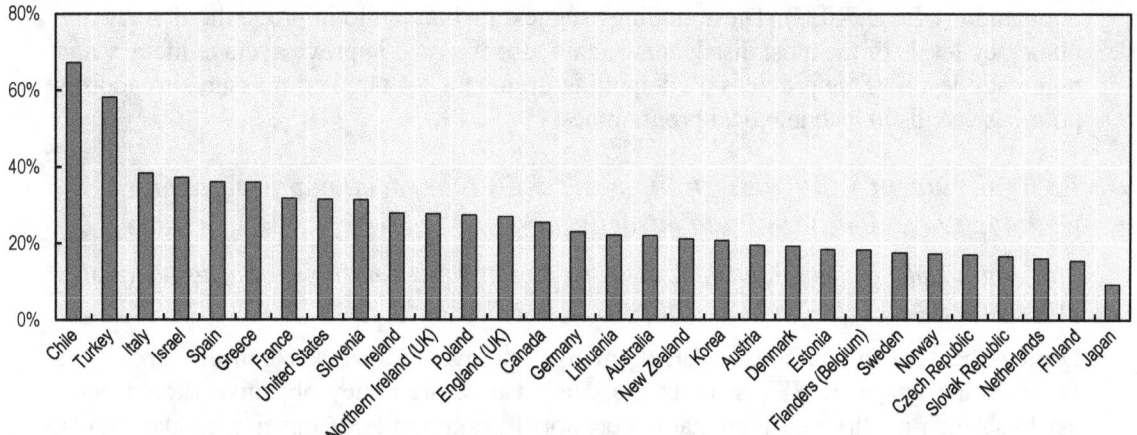

Source: OECD calculations based on OECD *Survey of Adult Skills (PIAAC)* (Database 2012, 2015), www.oecd.org/site/piaac/publicdataandanalysis.htm.

StatLink ⟶ http://dx.doi.org/10.1787/888933734968

Addressing low skills challenge could reduce inequalities

A wide distribution of numeracy/literacy skills is often related to greater social inequality (van Damme, 2013). Israel scores high both on skills dispersion and economic inequality as measured with income distribution. Israel's Gini index is much higher than the OECD average, and poverty rates are also high, especially among disadvantaged groups. Around 50% of the Arab population and Haredi populations live in poverty (OECD, 2018).

Policy argument 2. A large share of VET graduates lack basic skills

42% of young technological graduates have low skills

42% of young (16-40 year-olds) Israeli graduates from upper-secondary VET, accounting mainly for graduates from technological education, are low-skilled, a higher proportion than for their counterparts from many other countries (see Box 2.1 to see how upper-secondary VET was defined in this analysis).

There are big variations in the performance of VET graduates

Among young upper-secondary VET graduates, 176 score points separate the highest and the lowest 5% performers in numeracy, far above the OECD average of 139 score points (see Figure 5.4). While The Survey of Adult Skills, a product of the Programme for the International Assessment of Adult Competencies (PIAAC) data does explain why basic skills are so widely distributed, this wide dispersion may indicate that while in Israel there are many very successful schools or programmes, whose students are top performers, some schools or programmes are failing to provide the most basic skills to their students. This finding is consistent with the findings on the labour market outcomes from technological education as presented in Chapter 2.

Trade-off between quantity and quality

Analysis of the Programme for International Student Assessment (PISA) data suggests that in many countries inclusion of previously excluded – and mostly disadvantaged – populations in the education system improved the average performance of the whole population (OECD, 2017). These findings suggest that action to improve the literacy and numeracy levels of the most disadvantaged are also likely to improve average literacy and numeracy levels. This provides a compelling argument for targeted measures to address poor basic skills in technological programmes.

Policy argument 3. Building strong basic skills into vocational programmes would improve their status and attractiveness

The aim should be to establish a virtuous circle, attracting able students to quality programmes

During the OECD mission to Israel, many employers expressed concern about the deteriorating image of VET schools. To combat this, the policy objective should be to establish high-quality and high-status vocational programmes at upper-secondary level. Achieving this will require the creation of a virtuous circle, in which investment in the quality of a programme leads to strengthened labour market outcomes, and attracts more high ability candidates into the programme. This flow of high ability students will in turn further improve the status of the programme, and its attractiveness to employers, who will come to see it not only as high-quality education and training, but also as a means of recruiting able young students. This will further improve the labour market outcomes from the programme.

Strengthening the basic skills element of vocational programmes should help to realise this virtuous circle

Kick-starting this virtuous circle is a challenge, but one practical step to this end would be to build into all upper-secondary vocational programmes increased attention to basic skills of numeracy and literacy. This will provide skills needed in jobs, but also provide a vital foundation for progression into further and higher education, removing the risk that the programmes might be seen as dead ends.

Figure 5.4. In Israel, VET upper-secondary graduates have a low average and a wide spread of numeracy performance

Numeracy performance among 16-40 year-old VET graduates (highest qualification). In Israel upper-secondary VET refers to technological education.

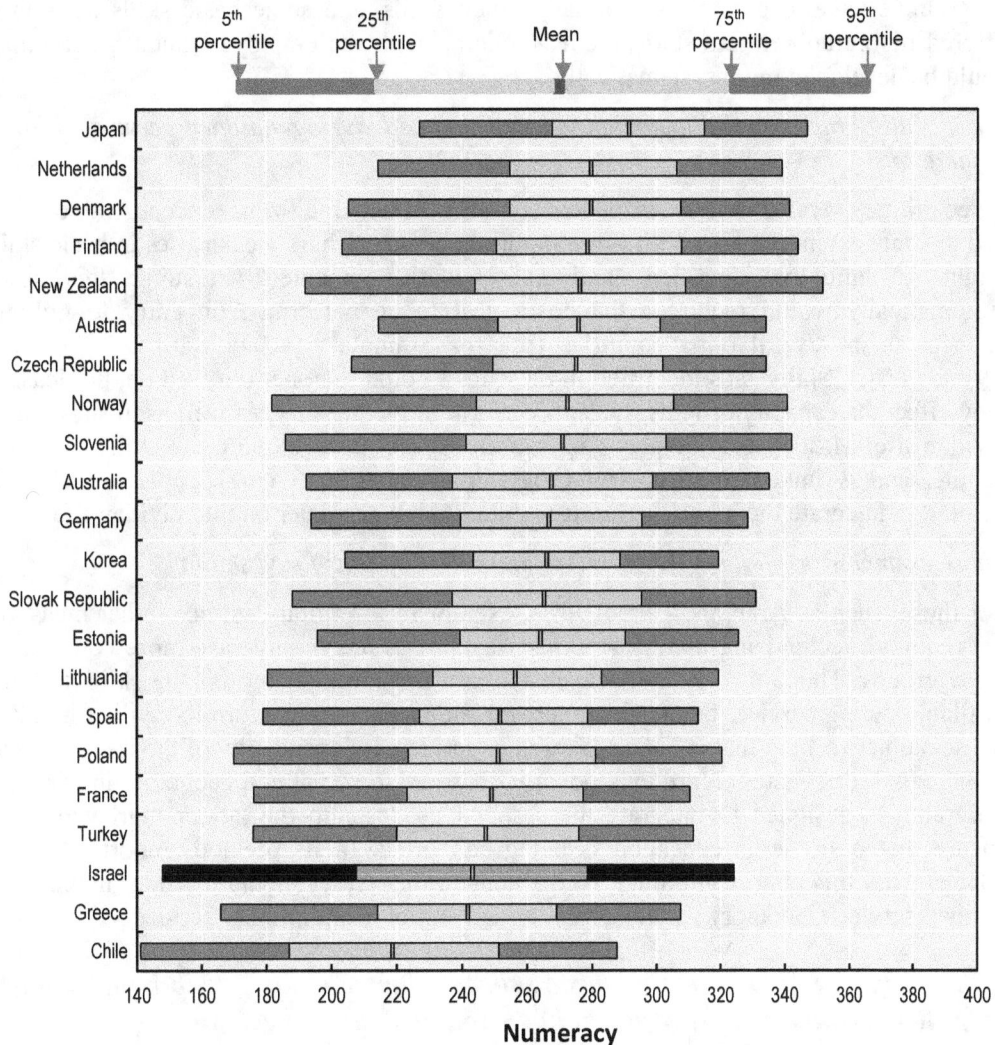

Note: England (United Kingdom), Flanders (Belgium), Italy, Northern Ireland, Sweden and the United States are excluded from analysis because in those countries it is impossible to identify VET graduates using the PIAAC database.
Source: OECD calculations based on OECD *Survey of Adult Skills (PIAAC)* (Database 2012, 2015), www.oecd.org/site/piaac/publicdataandanalysis.htm.

StatLink http://dx.doi.org/10.1787/888933734987

Policy argument 4. Israel can build on existing programmes catering to low-skilled

In Israel youth apprenticeships cater to young people performing poorly in regular schools

Youth apprentices in VET schools under the Ministry of Labour, Welfare and Social Services (MLWSS) are more often boys, from low socio-economic backgrounds, non-Jews, coming from special education classes in middle school, older than the cohort age, and with lower grades than students from MoE technological schools. More than one in four youth apprentices will drop out by the 12th grade, comparing to one out of 20 in MoE schools (Ben Rabi et al., forthcoming). Catering to these multiply disadvantaged young people requires a personalised approach including measures to address basic skills weaknesses, diagnosed in initial screening. For example, adult candidates for the Starter programme have to pass a test evaluating their skills, and some basic skills training is offered before apprentices start practical training with the employer. Such programmes could be developed more systematically.

Basic skills gaps can be identified and remediated during military service in some populations

Since military service in Israel is mandatory for most Israeli citizens (except Arab citizens and to some extent the Haredi) it is an important context where weaknesses in basic skills might be initially identified, and subsequently remedied. Pursuing this more systematically would require a diagnostic test to be performed on entry to military service, as in several other countries (see for example www.jobtestprep.co.uk/army-aptitude-tests). Skills gaps identified in these tests could then be followed up, not least as they affect the capacity of individuals to perform in the military, as well as in subsequent civilian life. Military service plays an important role in developing the skills of young people, and is linked to successful programmes targeting young people at risk, and helping to integrate them into the military initially, but also later on into civilian life.

Those exempt from military service need alternative options for upskilling

For those, such as Arab and Haredi Jews, exempt from military service, other measures are required, recognising that basic skills weaknesses are in any case more common in these groups. Those who do not pursue military service miss out on the skills training available during service, financial support for training on their return to civilian life, and the social networking that is linked to military service. Independently of the issue of basic skills, this set of factors represents potential barriers to social and economic integration. Programmes designed to integrate these social groups into the labour market need to ensure that basic skills education is being addressed. In its previous reports (OECD, 2018a), with this concern in mind, recommended that Israel should consider making the civilian service mandatory where there is an exemption from military service.

Policy argument 5. Addressing basic skills challenge among Arab Israelis and Haredi Jews would improve social inclusion and support economic growth

Arab Israelis are less likely to be in employment

Only 53% of the working age (25-65) Arab Israelis are employed. Among low-skilled Arabs, only 45% of them are employed, compared to 73% of the low-skilled Israeli Jews. Highly skilled Arabs are less likely to work than low-skilled Jews (see Figure 5.5). In addition PIAAC data shows that two similar Israeli citizens, in terms of gender, education level, family background and skills, but with different ethnic background (Arabs vs. Jews) receive significantly different wages, with Arabs being payed less.

Figure 5.5. Share of employed by skills and population group

25-65 year-olds

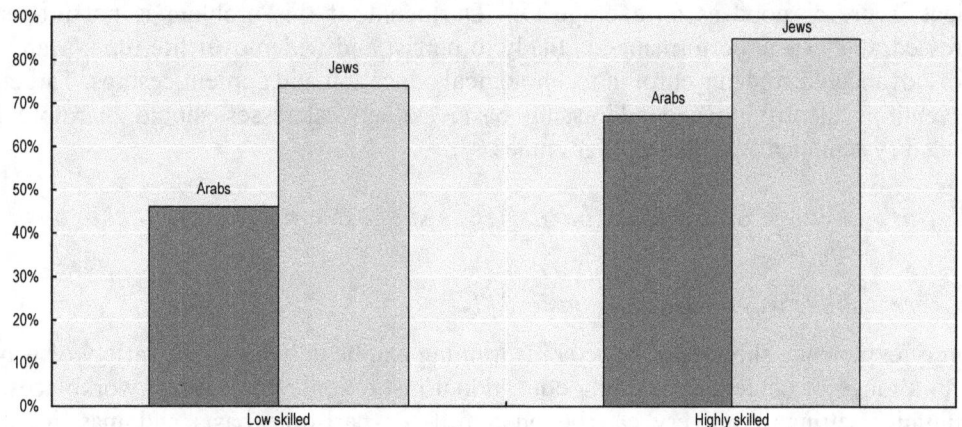

Source: OECD calculations based on OECD *Survey of Adult Skills (PIAAC)* (Database 2012, 2015), www.oecd.org/site/piaac/publicdataandanalysis.htm.

StatLink ⟶ http://dx.doi.org/10.1787/888933735006

Israeli labour market is highly segregated

On the one hand, there is a booming high-tech industry that offers attractive working conditions with high and growing wages. On the other, low-skilled disadvantaged workers are employed in blue-collar low-paid jobs. The high-tech sector, which attracts mostly high-skilled workers, is facing growing labour shortages, undermining its growth and competitiveness. Despite strong demand, the high-tech sector share of overall employment has been stuck at about 12% for a decade, and the sector is said to lack more than 10 000 engineers (Ministry of Economy, 2016). Still, only 2% of Arab Israelis work in this sector.

Without intervention the share of low-skilled labour in Israel may increase

The wave of migration from the former Soviet Union that increased the working-age population by 15% 25 years ago is approaching retirement age. At the same time, the share of workers from communities with low skills is increasing. Currently, Arab Israelis and Haredi Jews represent one-third of the population, but in 2059 they are projected to represent a half (Central Bureau of Statistics, 2017), mainly because of the increase of Haredi Jews. Official estimates show that for young adults (20-24 year-olds) the share of Arab Israelis and Haredi Jews will increase from around one-third currently to 55% by 2060 (OECD, 2018a). Consequently, if there is no improvement in basic skills of Haredi Jews and Arab Israelis, the Israeli labour workforce will be less skilled in the future than it is now.

Skills gap starts early on

Already at the pre-primary level Arab children participate less often in education than their Hebrew-speaking peers (CBS). At the age of 15, students who speak Arabic at home have significantly lower reading and mathematics skills than students speaking Hebrew at home, according to PISA. While young Israelis who speak Arabic at home score only 397 points in mathematics, much below OECD average of 490 points, Hebrew-speaking students score as good as an average OECD student. If this problem is not properly addressed, this gap in performance is likely to persist and widen over life time. Many of the disadvantaged students enrol in technological education and apprenticeships. Targeted interventions identifying and addressing basic skills weaknesses should therefore be included systematically in these programmes.

Policy argument 6. International experience suggest some tools to tackle basic skills

There are multiple ways of teaching basic skills

Country experience shows that basic skills training can be delivered in a variety of ways, and in a range of contexts, including educational institutions, job centres, workplaces or community settings. Delivery can be on a full- or part-time basis and may involve e-learning and blended learning. Teachers may hold a specific or a general teaching qualification, but most often they are (trained) volunteers (Tett and St.Clair, 2010). A major challenge is the lack of (particularly positive) evaluation evidence on the impact of those interventions.

Early intervention is the best approach

Ideally, strong basic skills should be established early on in life. Learning and development of skills is a dynamic process, in which successive stages of learning depends on skills acquired previously, particularly foundation skills such as literacy and numeracy (Heckman, 2008). There is some evidence that advantages of early intervention are even more important among at-risk groups, such as minorities (Bodovski and Youn, 2011). Although early intervention is the most effective approach, some adults at all ages will need basic skills training.

In the context of education and training for adults, systematic screening for literacy and numeracy difficulties should be used to identify adults in need of support, implementing the screening tactfully so that it is not seen as a barrier for those seeking entry to VET courses – perhaps after a few days of the course, so that it is not seen as a selective test or barrier to entry (Kis, 2010). Identifying students with weak basic skills, and supporting them systematically, will avoid the risk of them starting other forms of vocational training that they will not be able to manage without stronger basic skills.

Sometimes basic skills are best integrated into vocational training

There is some evidence that integrative learning blending basic skills teaching into occupation training leads to positive outcomes. Box 5.1 describes the I-BEST model that was introduced in the United States and that provides basic skills in the context of learning vocational subjects.

> **Box 5.1. Innovative initiatives addressing poor basic skills in US colleges**
>
> I-BEST is an innovative blend of basic skills with vocational education and training. Often too few students in adult basic skills programs upgrade their skills by transferring to post-secondary education. The Integrated Basic Education and Skills Training (I-BEST) was developed to improve entry rates to post-secondary career and technical education (CTE) in response to this challenge. Around 2% of basic skills students participated in I-BEST in the 2006-2008 period (Wachen et al., 2010). An I-BEST program combines basic skills teaching and professional training. Occupational training yields college credits that contribute to a certificate degree. These CTE courses can only be provided in occupations in demand on the labour market and leading to well paid jobs (Wachen et al., 2010). Combining basic skills with CTE content is facilitated by the availability of both types of program at community and technical colleges (I-BEST programmes are available in every community and technical college in Washington State). Individuals must score below a certain threshold on an adult skill test and qualify for adult basic education to participate in an I-BEST program. I-BEST students tend to perform better than non-participants and are more likely to have a high school or equivalent qualification.
>
> In the I-BEST program a teacher of basic skills and a teacher of professional-technical subject jointly instruct in the same classroom with at least a 50% overlap of instructional time (SBCTC, 2012). This increases the cost of provision and the state therefore funds I-BEST students at 1.75 times the normal per capita funding rate. From an individual point of view I-BEST programs are more expensive than adult basic education as students pay for the college-level portion of the I-BEST program. This might prevent some adults from participating as many I-BEST students are from low-income families and cannot afford tuition in college-level classes (Wachen et al., 2010). Students can receive financial support from federal (Pell grant) and state sources (State need Grant and opportunity Grant) but as reported by Wachen et al., (2010) many students interested in I-BEST do not qualify for this aid. Proving eligibility for the financial aid can sometimes be complicated and deter students from applying.
>
> A few studies measuring the impact of I-BEST found that I-BEST students earn more credits and are more likely to complete a degree than a comparable group of basic skill students not participating in the program. Evidence on the link between participation in I-BEST and earnings is less conclusive, although this might be due to changing economic conditions and the US and Washington State economy entering the recession (Jenkins et al, 2010).
>
> *Source*: SBCTC (2012), *Integrated Basic Education and Skills Training (I-BEST)*, www.sbctc.ctc.edu/college/e_integratedbasiceducationandskillstraining.aspx (accessed February 2013); Wachen J., D. Jenkins and M. Van Noy (2010), "How I-BEST Works: Findings from a Field Study of Washington State's Integrated basic Education and Skills Training Program", CCRC, New York; Jenkins D., M. Zeidenberg and G. Kienzl (2010), "Educational Outcomes of I-BEST, Washington State Community and Technical College System's Integrated Basic Education and Skills Training Program: Findings from a Multivariate Analysis", *Working Paper* No. 16, CCRC in Kuczera, M. and S. Field (2013), *Skills beyond School Review of the United States*, OECD Reviews of Vocational Education and Training, http://dx.doi.org/10.1787/9789264202153-en.

New technologies may also help to improve the basic skills of adults

In Israel, 87% of adults use a computer in everyday life (OECD, 2018b), around the average of OECD participating countries. Among Arab Israelis, use of computers in everyday life remains high (80%). Darling-Hammond, Zielezinski and Goldman (2014) reviewing more than 70 recent studies, found that technology coupled with a strategic policy approach could successfully be used to support underprivileged students, to help them strengthen their understanding, close skill gaps, and recoup prior experiences of failure. So, one option is to build e-learning of different types into vocational programmes, with a focus on literacy and numeracy. This requires experimentation and evaluation.

References

Bank of Israel (n.d.), "Excerpt from the Fiscal Survey and collection of research issues: Basic skills of workers in Israel and industry productivity", 2016, www.boi.org.il/en/NewsAndPublications/PressReleases/Pages/19-07-2016.aspx.

Bodovski, K. and M. Youn (2011), "The long term effects of early acquired skills and behaviors on young children's achievement in literacy and mathematics", *Journal of Early Childhood Research*, http://dx.doi.org/10.1177/1476718X10366727.

Central Bureau of Statistics (2017), "Projections for Israel population until 2065. Tables and diagrams", www.cbs.gov.il/reader/newhodaot/tables_template_eng.html?hodaa=201701138.

Ben Rabi D., L. King, D., T. (forthcoming), "Apprenticeship and Work-based Learning in Israel".

van Damme, D. (2013), "How closely is the distribution of skills related to countries' overall level of social inequality and economic prosperity?", *OECD Education Working Papers*, No. 105, OECD Publishing, Paris, http://dx.doi.org/10.1787/5jxvd5rk3tnx-en.

Darling-Hammond, L., M. Zielezinski and S. Goldman (2014), *Using Technology to Support At-Risk Students' Learning*, Stanford Center for Opportunity Policy in Education, https://edpolicy.stanford.edu/sites/default/files/scope-pub-using-technology-report.pdf.

Heckman, J. (2008), "Schools, skills, and synapses", *Economic Inquiry*, Vol. 46/3, pp. 289-324, http://dx.doi.org/10.1111/j.1465-7295.2008.00163.x.

Jenkins D., M. Zeidenberg and G. Kienzl (2010), "Educational Outcomes of I-BEST, Washington State Community and Technical College System's Integrated Basic Education and Skills Training Program: Findings from a Multivariate Analysis", *Working Paper* No. 16, CCRC.

Kis, V. (2010), *OECD Reviews of Vocational Education and Training: A Learning for Jobs Review of Ireland 2010*, OECD Reviews of Vocational Education and Training, OECD Publishing, Paris, http://dx.doi.org/10.1787/9789264113848-en.

Ministry of Economy (2016), *Israel Innovation Authority Report*, Ministry of Economy, Jerusalem.

OECD (2018a), *OECD Economic Surveys: Israel 2018*, OECD Publishing, Paris, http://dx.doi.org/10.1787/eco_surveys-isr-2018-en.

OECD (2018b), *Survey of Adult Skills (PIAAC)* (Database 2012, 2015), www.oecd.org/site/piaac/publicdataandanalysis.htm.

OECD (2017), "Does the quality of learning outcomes fall when education expands to include more disadvantaged students?", *PISA in Focus*, No. 75, OECD Publishing, Paris, http://dx.doi.org/10.1787/06c8a756-en.

OECD (2016), *Skills Matter: Further Results from the Survey of Adult Skills*, OECD Skills Studies, OECD Publishing, Paris, http://dx.doi.org/10.1787/9789264258051-en.

Grotlüschen, A., et al. (2016), "Adults with low proficiency in literacy or numeracy", *OECD Education Working Papers*, No. 131, OECD Publishing, Paris, http://dx.doi.org/10.1787/5jm0v44bnmnx-en.

SBCTC (2012), *Integrated Basic Education and Skills Training (I-BEST)*, www.sbctc.ctc.edu/college/e_integratedbasiceducationandskillstraining.aspx (accessed February 2013).

Tett, L. and R. St.Clair (2010), "Adult literacy education", in *International Encyclopaedia of Education*, Elsevier, http://dx.doi.org/10.1016/B978-0-08-044894-7.00019-1.

Wachen J., D. Jenkins and M. Van Noy (2010), *How I-BEST Works: Findings from a Field Study of Washington State's Integrated Basic Education and Skills Training Program*, CCRC, New York.

ORGANISATION FOR ECONOMIC CO-OPERATION AND DEVELOPMENT

The OECD is a unique forum where governments work together to address the economic, social and environmental challenges of globalisation. The OECD is also at the forefront of efforts to understand and to help governments respond to new developments and concerns, such as corporate governance, the information economy and the challenges of an ageing population. The Organisation provides a setting where governments can compare policy experiences, seek answers to common problems, identify good practice and work to co-ordinate domestic and international policies.

The OECD member countries are: Australia, Austria, Belgium, Canada, Chile, the Czech Republic, Denmark, Estonia, Finland, France, Germany, Greece, Hungary, Iceland, Ireland, Israel, Italy, Japan, Korea, Latvia, Luxembourg, Mexico, the Netherlands, New Zealand, Norway, Poland, Portugal, the Slovak Republic, Slovenia, Spain, Sweden, Switzerland, Turkey, the United Kingdom and the United States. The European Union takes part in the work of the OECD.

OECD Publishing disseminates widely the results of the Organisation's statistics gathering and research on economic, social and environmental issues, as well as the conventions, guidelines and standards agreed by its members.

www.ingramcontent.com/pod-product-compliance
Lightning Source LLC
Chambersburg PA
CBHW082353220526
45470CB00008B/2726